INSPIRE YOUR KIDS TO GREATNESS

Other Books by Jerry Johnston

Why Suicide?
*Going All the Way: The Real World of
    Teens and Sex*
*The Edge of Evil: The Rise of Satanism in
    North America*
*It's Killing Our Kids: Teenage Alcohol Abuse
    and Addiction*
The Last Days of Planet Earth
*Who's Listening? What Our Kids Are Trying
    To Tell Us*

Videos by Jerry Johnston

Life Exposé
Why Suicide?
The Edge of Evil
It's Killing Our Kids
The Cutting Edge
AIDS Among Teens
Commitment: It's Time To Make Up Your Mind
Kids 'n' Gangs
Who's Listening?

INSPIRE YOUR KIDS TO GREATNESS

How Parents Can Nurture God's Next Generation

JERRY JOHNSTON

ZondervanPublishingHouse
Grand Rapids, Michigan

A Division of HarperCollinsPublishers

Inspire Your Kids to Greatness
How Parents Can Nurture God's Next Generation
Copyright © 1993 by Jerry Johnston
All rights reserved

Published by Zondervan Publishing House
Grand Rapids, Michigan 49530

Library of Congress Cataloging-in-Publication Data

Johnston, Jerry, 1959-
    Inspire your kids to greatness : how parents can nurture God's
next generation / by Jerry Johnston.
      p. cm.
    ISBN 0-310-57861-2 (pbk. : alk. paper)
    1. Parenting—Religious aspects—Christianity. 2. Parents—
Religious life. I. Title.
    BV4526.2.J57   1993
    248.8'45—dc20   93–27151
                                                                   CIP

All Scripture quotations, unless otherwise indicated, are taken from the *Holy Bible, New International Version®. NIV®*. Copyright © 1973, 1978, 1984 by International Bible Society. Used by permission of Zondervan Publishing House. All rights reserved.

Printed in the United States of America

Edited by Lyn Cryderman
Cover design by David Marty
Cover photo by Don Smetzer, Tony Stone Images

93 94 95 96 97 / DH / 5 4 3 2 1

This edition is printed on acid-free paper and meets the American National Standards Institute Z39.48 standard.

To My Parents, John and Joyce Johnston—

To my dear dad, who has truly been my inspiration to strive for true greatness. Did you ever think that from those many years of coaching me and encouraging me to do better, that through all those hard lessons there would one day come a book?

To my wonderful mom, who has always believed in me. From the first time I came home at age eighteen and told you I was going to record a live album, you would always respond, "Jerry, I don't doubt it for a minute."

I love you, Mom and Dad.

Contents

To obtain other materials by Jerry Johnston or receive a free products catalog, call or write:

Jerry Johnston Association
P. O. Box 12193
Overland Park, KS 66282-2193
Phone: (913) 492-2066
Fax: (913) 492-3768

Introduction

This book has been such a rewarding project. In my previous works I have brought to light many of the problems facing youth and parents in society today.

Now, in this book I have listed what I feel are the essential ingredients to inspire our kids. In my extensive travels over the years, addressing and listening to millions of young people, I have met some students who really had it together. And there were reasons why.

Many of them had a mom and/or dad or some other adult who inspired them to greatness. The ingredients that have led such children to greatness have received little attention by my own ministry, my messages, the church today, and society in general. I hope this book changes that. I hope you'll begin seeing ways by which you can inspire good kids to become great.

The principles within these pages are born out of personal experience. I came to Jesus Christ as a teenager entering the ninth grade. On Sunday morning at our church after hearing me share my newfound faith, my dad and mom made the same decision just three days later. The Johnston family, which had been so plagued with problems, suddenly became communicative, harmonious, even happy. What a miracle!

To think that just eleven weeks earlier I had been checked out of St. Luke's Hospital weighing sixty-eight pounds, suicidal, and afraid of life. How could I aspire to greatness?

A unique cohesion soon developed between my dad and me, both of us brand-new Christians. He became my coach in life, and quickly we began to grow spiritually together. I started a youth club at the public school I attended. In one year the club members introduced 30 percent of the school to Christ; over two hundred students made decisions for Christ. Through the challenge of a local youth ministry, I started speaking in small Bible clubs and churches while still in high school.

On every occasion possible I tape-recorded my message and took it home to Dad. Up in the "Big D" (my bedroom), he would critique every minute, almost even to my inhaling and exhaling! This valuable time was more than just focusing on how to be an effective communicator; it was also the avenue for Dad's repeated lessons to me on greatness.

How I relish those many times with Dad in the Big D. They set my spiritual moorings and instilled in me the challenge to reach for something great with my life. It was Dad who met with me privately before every important meeting or conference I had, teaching me the art of negotiation, the power of self-confidence, and the wonder of giving God preeminence in my life. He really believed that when your heart is truly right with God and your disciplines are in place, the sky is the limit. And I learned to believe that.

Some people believe that greatness is success, fame, or material advantage. Others confuse it with wealth and the accolades of this world. But true greatness transcends position or rank. In the pages of this book I will explain greatness and how our kids can get it. The following chapters are a compendium of how to imbue our children with greatness principles that will make them victorious, principles that they will pass on to their kids.

> Jerry Johnston
> Kansas City

1

Understanding Greatness

The word *great* is used very loosely in society today.

We hear about great entertainers, great athletes, great politicians, great businessmen and women, and even great preachers, but in our contemporary culture, the definition of greatness is generally reduced to having great wealth, fame, and the ability to influence vast numbers of people.

True greatness transcends social and economic status. In my extensive travels the last fourteen years, I have met young people and adults who aspired to and achieved greatness, some who were rich and others who were poor, some educated and some uneducated, some renowned and some living in almost total obscurity. And I have met a number of so-called great students and adults who, I was convinced, didn't have a clue to what true greatness is all about.

I hope this book helps you more clearly identify the target for your children—true greatness. But more important, once you've identified the target, you still have to help your children learn how to shoot, when to shoot, and with what to shoot at the target of greatness.

Greatness on God's terms

It was Christ himself who made a crucial connection between children and greatness. "I tell you the truth, unless you change and become like little children, you will never enter the kingdom of heaven. Therefore, whoever humbles himself like this child is the greatest in the kingdom of heaven" (Matt. 18:3–4).

Christ also said: ". . . Whoever practices and teaches [God's] commands will be called great in the kingdom of heaven" (Matt. 5:19).

These verses make at least three things clear.

First, parents shouldn't feel guilty about wanting their children to achieve greatness. After all, Christ set greatness as a desirable goal for all believers.

Second, there is a biblical pattern that leads to greatness.

Third, biblical greatness is not necessarily the same as greatness by worldly standards. Jesus said that those who follow the biblical paths to greatness—among them (1) becoming like children, (2) humbling oneself, and (3) keeping and teaching God's commands—will indeed be called great. And just where will they be called great? In the kingdom of heaven.

As Christian parents, we are aspiring for our children to become great—no doubt about it, but we want children who are great in God's kingdom and under God's terms.

Your role as a parent essentially is to set up your children so that they can attain greatness. Don't try to "make" them great. You can't do it for them even though—given your experience and wisdom—you feel that you have learned how to do things that your children are just learning how to do; you have learned what in life to avoid and what to embrace. And you want to help them! Resist that urge and, instead, equip them to become great on their own.

Equipping our children to paint their own pictures

Marshall Bouldin is one of America's greatest portrait artists. He's painted numerous dignitaries including presidents and governors. His studio is nestled in the dusty, hot Delta of Mississippi. Big windows let in the warm Delta light that splashes onto the paintings he is working on. It's perfect light for an artist, he says.

These days, Marshall often shares his studio with his youngest son, Jason. The two love each other deeply. More than that, they have immense respect for each other. When Jason decided during his college years that he wanted to paint, he asked his father to help bring him along and to supplement his more formal studies on the East Coast.

At times Jason paints alongside his renowned father, sharing that same Delta light in his father's studio. They critique each other's work. They offer each other comments.

But there are some times when the master's seasoned eye is just plain and simply much better than his talented son's. Marshall says that there are times he is watching his son work when suddenly the younger Bouldin will get frustrated. He is stumped. More than that, the young buck will start demeaning his work in process. He even gets to the point where he wants to trash his work and start all over.

In one particular instance, recalls the older Bouldin, "Jason was almost to the point he wanted to run. I thought, *I've got to guide this boy. I've got to solve his problem. . . .* I was bleeding for him. . . . He had a great painting there he almost wanted to destroy. And I can't go up there and paint it for him."

Don't we all feel the same way during different times

in our work of parenting our children? Like Marshall Bouldin, we see our children's abilities. We praise their skills and help hone them. But we have to let our children paint their own pictures. And at times, how hard it is to stand back and watch as they miss a stroke here or there!

Like the older Bouldin with his son, we must restrain ourselves. Our hope is that the painting skills we have taught our children, coupled with their innate abilities, will win the day. So it is with raising a child for greatness. Our job as parents is to instill in our children the necessities and equip them to incorporate those necessities into their own pool of natural abilities. As Christians, we are confident that our God will also intercede to lead our children to godly greatness.

There are many reasons why I am so interested in greatness. After having spoken in over 3000 public schools, I have heard enough disaster stories to last me a lifetime. I've talked firsthand with the many students who have had no inspiration at all. There were many days after having spoken to 5000 to 7000 young people in a day and after having interacted with several children close up that I was left in a deep depression at the sadness of it all. *If only these valuable, irreplaceable kids were inspired to reach for something greater*, I thought.

Down the itinerant trail that I travel, I also have been cheerfully interrupted with youth who were the exact opposite of the deteriorating kids I encounter. This second group of teens was excited; they had direction; their countenance exuded inspiration. They were reaching for the stars! Why? Virtually every one of them had someone inspiring them to greatness.

Often it was their parents. However, in some instances it was not. Some of these young people had faced insurmountable obstacles, yet they valiantly weathered storm after storm. I feel deeply led to highlight these winners who live in an age where so many youth are being snuffed out far before reaching their potential. Instead of magnifying the problem, we must magnify the solution. We must give our kids the principles that will lead them to something spectacular in their lives.

I also am deeply concerned about inspiring kids to greatness, because I myself am a parent. Beyond the multitude of words I speak into a microphone each year are my own kids, who hold the scrutinizing yardstick to my own ability and integrity as a parent and inspirer. Somewhat reluctantly, I have included in this book a few of the challenges and problems that my wife, Christie, and I have faced with our children.

Like any other parent, I know how some wrenching problems with our children can drive us mothers and fathers to our knees. In fact, the key motivator for many parents' decisions to return to God and faith has often been concern for the welfare of their children. As Kenneth Woodward wrote in *Newsweek*, "Having transformed American society as they marched toward middle age, the nation's baby boomers are leading a return to organized religion. Much of the revival is fueled by the boomers' experiencing parenthood: They want a place for their children to acquire solid values." We realize sooner or later that the job of parenting is beyond us. We need higher power.

Getting on our knees

Obviously, supernatural motivation fits in and is inseparable to parents' inspiring their kids to greatness.

Let's begin with a prayer, a specific petition to God to provide your child with "discretion and understanding."

Next to the prayer for salvation, no prayer may be of more inspiration for your children than one for wisdom and understanding, the very sort of prayer that King David offered to God for his son Solomon.

King David prayed in 1 Chronicles 22:12, "May the Lord give you [Solomon] wisdom and understanding." David prayed for Solomon!

Almighty God heard this prayer for blessing by David.

Then King David died.

Solomon became king.

Though time had passed, God still remembered David's original prayer for his son. And God answered! In 2 Chronicles 1:7, God asked Solomon what he might give the young king. Solomon replied in verse 10, "Give me wisdom and knowledge."

It happened. David had prayed for Solomon's greatness to be accomplished by granting his son a heart that would seek wisdom and understanding. Then Solomon bore the fruit of his father's prayer. God answered David.

Let me emphasize that this is the finest example in the Bible of a parent's offering a specific prayer for greatness. The relationship was triangular:

1. David prayed to God.
2. God heard the prayer and inspired Solomon.
3. Unknowingly, Solomon prayed for the answer to his father's specific prayer.

This biblical example illustrates the supernatural elements of our calling as parents. What an encouragement! Such is the adventure we are about to embark on. Let's get on with inspiring our kids to godly greatness.

First, we'll take a glimpse at a few people who were ready and usable when God called and who offered their skills and abilities and hearts to God, who in turn made them great. And by the way, let these stories inspire you, too!

2

Biblical Characteristics of Greatness

The Bible offers several examples of how God took certain "ready and usable" people and ignited certain strong character qualities within them to carry them on to greatness. Let's look at a few of those characteristics.

Trust. One of the all-time best personifications of greatness was a man who was sold into slavery by his brothers when he was only seventeen. Joseph had committed no evil acts toward his brethren. He had given them no cause to make him suffer in exile from his family as a slave to other men, and he was loved dearly by his father. He had a servant's heart toward his brothers and was a very courageous young man in the face of suffering. Such trials could have caused him to cave in to life.

But there is something unique about a person who aspires to greatness. He trusts. And he does not cave in to life's "injustices." His character is strong enough to carry him through all of the unjust, negative experiences in life. His determination to press forward by trusting in his God enables him to make the right decisions. They propel him forward to the point of greatness, to that time when God is ready to use him for great things.

This seventeen-year-old lad had started developing his character in life. He was ready and usable when God called. As a slave he was assigned a menial work that he

honored by his effort, never showing signs of discourage-
ment. Read about Joseph in the Bible. He succeeded to
greatness because he trusted the vision of greatness God
had given him. He never stopped trusting and believing.
And in the end, he saved his people from disaster.

Repentance. Zacchaeus cheated everyone. He cheated
even his own people. He extorted from them. He was
evil. He was scorned and loathed by everyone. He had
persons working under him who did the same kind of
evil to other good people. But he was the chief of them—
the chief cheater—and he was hated by all.

Yet he achieved greatness.

He was in the top of a sycamore tree, trying to view
the one he had heard so much about. Finally, the Great
Teacher arrived near him and said, "Come down; today I
will be with you in your house."

The evil person was picked out of this mammoth
crowd of onlookers to be the one with whom God would
dwell. And what was this little man's response? "Yes. I
want to change. Come to my home. Dwell with me.
Furthermore, I'll give back four times more than what I
extorted from the people." Zacchaeus succeeded to
greatness by being ready and usable and repentant when
God called.

Confidence. Deborah was one of the judges of Israel,
and people came to her for sound counsel and decisions.
She commanded Barak to take ten thousand men and go
up in battle against Sisera, but Barak would go only if
Deborah went with him. He lacked the confidence of
Deborah.

Deborah said that she would go with Barak, but that if
she did, it would not be for his honor, because God
would surely deliver Sisera into the hands of a woman.

Israel had battled Sisera and his army before but had not overcome them. Nevertheless, this battle took place with Deborah as the leader. Sisera led his troops in retreat and eventually went into the tent of a woman whose name was Jael, who took a nail and hammer while he was sleeping and killed him.

This left the Canaanite army without a leader, so they were easily followed and destroyed by Barak and his army. And then Deborah sang a song of praise to God for the victory.

God's call to greatness is for those who have confidence rooted in a relationship with him. Deborah was confident. The song of Deborah is prophetic. A significant characteristic for attaining greatness is the confident belief that banishes the fear of man and praises the fear of God.

Commitment. When a widowed mother prepared to return to her homeland from the land of her one-time captors, she advised her two daughters-in-law, who also had been widowed, to remain in their country and seek happiness among that country's men and their pagan gods. One daughter-in-law did so, but the other one, Ruth, because of her great respect and affection for her mother-in-law, Naomi, elected to go with her and to follow Naomi's God.

Ruth pledged her consecration sevenfold, by saying, "Don't urge me to leave you or to turn back from you. Where you go I will go and where you stay I will stay. Your people will be my people and your God my God. Where you die, I will die, and there I will be buried. May the Lord deal with me, be it ever so severely, if anything but death separates you and me" (Ruth 1:16–17).

Her love for her mother-in-law and her willingness to go to a strange land and to live with strange people was evidence of a total surrender to God and trust in his provision.

In fact, while her mother-in-law at one point accused God of making her life bitter, the daughter-in-law worshiped God and desired to serve, trust, and obey him. The two returned to Judah and to the roots of the Hebrew faith, where Ruth was destined by God to become wedded to Boaz, a mighty man of wealth, and to become a part of the direct line of the coming Messiah.

Whose plan was this for Ruth's life? It was God's plan! Who was the implementer of the plan for Ruth's life? It was her mother-in-law, Naomi, who brought Ruth and Boaz together as man and wife. God's plan for our life of greatness is to place opportunities for faith in our path. If we respond, he will do the rest. We must only be committed against all odds like a Ruth. Sooner or later— and we don't know which it will be—God will bring along our opportunities for greatness.

Courage. Esther was brought to the king's house to enter the first beauty contest recorded in history. It was to determine the most beautiful and talented virgin in all the king's empire. The competition was great because officers in all of the provinces throughout the empire gathered together all of the fair young virgins.

The time came for the decision of the king. The young orphan pleased him. The king loved her above all of the others. Yet in everyone's life, including beauty queens and kings, there is always a villain—a person who is trying to defeat the cause, purpose, and mission of the person who is trying to attain godly greatness. In the case of this queen, the villain was working to exterminate her race of people. But while in each person's life villains do appear, so does the hand the of the almighty God.

You probably know the rest of the story. After

learning of the impending destruction of her people, the queen determined to enter the court of her king even though to do so without invitation customarily meant death. Said the queen, "If I perish, I perish."

This display of courage, followed by a determination to act, is a basic requirement for greatness.

The king received his queen. In the end, the villain, Haman, who sought the destruction of the queen's people, was himself destroyed. The queen's uncle, Mordecai, was elevated to power as second in command in the empire. The race was saved from execution, as is the genealogical plan for the coming Messiah, the Savior of the world. And the queen, Esther, has been memorialized by her people each year since and will be until the end of time.

Faith. The little maid was from Israel. She had been brought captive out of her land. She waited on her mistress and her mistress's husband, Naaman, who himself was an honorable man and a leper.

The little maid could have been very angry and vindictive because she and her people were captives of the Syrian enemies. She could have been outraged, but she wasn't. She viewed Naaman as a hurting man who needed healing. And she knew the Great Healer who could help him. Her faith made her believe that her God could heal Naaman, so she told her mistress about God's prophet.

The little maid is a wonderful example of faith as the essential characteristic of greatness. She had aspired to greatness, and her faith enabled her to be content in her position as a captive, and to encourage Naaman to seek healing. Second Kings 5 portrays the entire story of Naaman, who eventually received healing by obeying the prophet Elisha's command to bathe in the Jordan

River. He was healed, and the little maid became great in the eyes of God. She led Naaman to the throne of grace.

Anyone—regardless of age or position—who has faith even the size of a mustard seed, can attain to greatness. Even "little people" like a seemingly insignificant maid. Have faith and teach your children faith as well!

Meekness. Why would God select a meek man like Moses to lead all of his people out of Egypt into the Promised Land? God knew beforehand of all of the murmurings of the Israelites. He knew of the forty years it would take for them to complete the journey. God knew all of the temptations and failures of the Israelites. God knew beforehand all of the demands and discourtesies that the people would have for their leader.

God uses the meek leaders in the long run because they are the ones who have the long view for greatness. They are men and women who will always ultimately come back to him and seek him and obey him instead of seeking their own way. He cannot use the bashers, the proud, or the haughty. God's ways are paradoxically different. God inspired Moses to greatness through his meekness.

Humility. No one wants to be number two. To be number two assures one of "standing in the shadow" of the number-one person. The world says that being number one means being great. But what does God say?

The number-two person is generally viewed as a lame duck, a wimp, a person without much ability, not capable. Everyone walks toward but past the number-two man to address the numero uno.

The number-two person is present but only to be the errand boy, the gofer, the handyman.

But some number-two men and women are different—

especially when they are in God's hands. They are students-in-residence, always serving. And they are always learning from the number-one man. They are in place for the purpose of becoming qualified to take over the number-one position some day.

They are humble.

One of these number-two men was Joshua.

Joshua, the number-two man, was appointed by Moses to be the number-one leader. Joshua became number one in full charge to take the children of Israel over the Jordan River into the Promised Land. What an awesome responsibility. God needed just the right man who had all of the experience of being number two, a man who was not prideful.

Patience. Job was the greatest of all the men of the East. There was no one like him in the earth, an upright man—one who feared God and avoided evil. Though he had lost everything, he did not complain.

His wife and friends mocked him, yet he did not complain. Was Job great because he was rich? Was Job great because he was wise? Ultimately, Job's greatness was defined in another way. We view him as the model of patience. Could Job have possibly known that his life would become an endless memorial to godly patience? Job was ready and usable and patient, and God made him great.

Would you know greatness if you saw it?

Some of us may not realize even our own greatness in God's eyes. For that matter, it may be even harder to spot the greatness God is molding in our children.

But if we make them ready and usable and fill them

with godly character, beliefs, and values, then we can rest assured that God can and will take it from there.

So how do we make them ready and usable and full of godly character? We inspire them to it! Let's look more closely at what it means to inspire and how to inspire.

3

Understanding Inspiration

One of the remarkable examples of how to inspire your kids to greatness is theologian/philosopher/pastor Jonathan Edwards. He and his wife, Sarah, raised twelve kids. And even though both parents were deceased when their youngest child was eight years old, the children faithfully carried on their godly heritage through their parents' original inspiration.

One-hundred-forty-two years after the death of their parents (1758), the Edwards's descendants had produced: one-hundred foreign missionaries; platoons of full-time Christian workers; thirteen college presidents; sixty-five professors; one-hundred lawyers; thirty judges; sixty-six physicians; one dean of a medical school; eighty holders of public office; and one vice-president of the United States.

This wonderful heritage confirms one of Jonathan Edwards's most meaningful and significant sayings that "every family ought to be . . . a little church; consecrated to Christ . . . and family education and order are some of the chief means of grace."

Inspiration is the most misunderstood and yet unique motivating force known to humankind. It can't be bought with money. It can't be counterfeited. It can't be borrowed or loaned. It can't be accomplished with bribery or promises. It is as genuine and sincere as is truth. When inspiration kisses love, it produces a result that is immeasurable and unimaginable. It will cause an effect that, without wings, will soar with the highest eagles and almost reach heaven. It will sail oceans without a wind.

The meaning of *inspire*

Many parents try to coerce their kids. Theirs is a system of ten more commandments. As long as the children are under their hand it may work, but frequently, even then it doesn't. Don't drive them toward greatness. Inspire them. There is a big difference.

The *Webster's Ninth New Collegiate Dictionary* offers this definition of the word *inspire* : "To influence, move, or guide by divine or supernatural inspiration; to exert an animating, enlivening, or exalting influence on." That is what we as parents ought to be about! Divinely guiding and arousing and stimulating our children toward creativity and action that leads to godly greatness. There is another dictionary definition of *inspire*: "To push, propel, or press onward forcibly; to repulse by authority or force; to force to work, usually excessively; to force into or from a particular act or state."

You get the idea.

What parent doesn't recall seeing at one time or another an over-eager baseball parent who pushes little Johnny to excel according to that parent's own warped definition of the word?

I once heard a true story of a Little Leaguer who was tall, lanky, and had a faceful of acne. His physical appearance made him a little insecure, but the boy could hit a baseball.

One night during a game he stepped up to the plate and took the signals from his coach at third base. Then he promptly smacked the first pitch over the centerfield fence.

With a huge grin, the boy trotted around the bases as he received the congratulations of opposing teammates. But when he got to home plate, there was the coach, who promptly chewed him out for not having caught his signal to bunt!

That is a sad example of an adult's driving a child toward his own preconceived and warped notion of greatness, which in this case was defined as mastering all the nuances of baseball. The joy of the boy's innate hitting greatness was snuffed out in the nitpicking process. This was not inspired. This was driven.

Inspiring our kids to greatness begins with us, the parents. Unlike the Little League coach just mentioned, there must be virtue, character, and example in our life for our kids to follow. Moreover, we must have spiritual fiber. Everything that embodies God should be in our lives. As Christian parents we are more equipped to meet this challenge if we follow closely the precepts in God's Word.

The search for inspiration

Inspiration, then, begins with *us*. It is a perfect mirror of our spiritual depth or shallowness. George Whitefield's old adage is so true: "We can preach the Gospel no further than we have experienced its own power in our lives."

We can parent, or inspire, no further than the quality and commitment of our own lives.

Inspiration isn't something packaged in preweighed, prefabbed bundles. It sometimes comes in massive outpourings, much like the finale of a great symphony. Or it can slip out in the most minute doses, almost like a mouse peeking out of its hole. Inspiration exudes from a committed, accomplished body, be it a body of fine musicians, a body of top-notch athletes, or the body of one man or woman whose life of devoted prayer rubs off on others.

Sometimes—in fact, oftentimes—inspiration exudes from someone without that person's even knowing it, in the process of simply going about one's business before God. Just being faithful. Just being real. But in the process, his or her life may change another's for good— and for the better. Such is the story of inspiration that I am about to share with you.

A young man named George felt like a prisoner in his own home as he waited for his father to arrive. Finally, the door swung open. His father stomped in. He roared, "You young jailbird, you don't have the decency to hide."

Young George's response was, "You might have paid my fine a lot faster because the meals in that German jail were terrible."

"What did I raise in my child, a common thief?" his father replied in total exasperation.

After this experience, George became a carefree reveler, hiking, drinking Swiss wine, diving into mountain pools, tumbling down grassy fields, and sleeping until he felt like going on.

But eventually George found his way to a series of religious meetings. At one gathering he observed Brother Kayser kneeling on a wooden floor and praying to God to bless souls and to be present. George stared in fascination. He noticed that when Brother Kayser prayed, it really seemed that he was talking to someone who had somehow moved into the room and stood in great power. Never before had George seen a man kneel to pray.

He was inspired by the moment!

Finally, it struck him why Kayser kneeled to pray. He felt that the old man wanted to tell God that he was humble and human. What an unusual man!

For years, ever since confirmation, George had known the facts of the Atonement and had understood perfectly that Jesus Christ had died on a cross to save a guilty world. But to George this Atonement had not really lived because, to George, God had not really lived.

Everything changed when George saw old Brother Kayser kneeling to pray. So much so that the next day George kneeled to pray. The floor felt uncomfortable and cold to his knees. It didn't matter. He prayed while kneeling. He thought, *When you kneel like this, low before the highest One, meek before the omnipotent One, then God is real!*

George exclaimed, "At last, God, I am yours!"

He stayed on his knees for almost a half hour. Then he got up a little woodenly and sat down on the bed. He knew that something wonderful had happened to him. He was reborn spiritually. It was all because one man showed with every muscle in his body that he worshiped, feared, and really knew the living God.

All of a sudden George said that Christianity seemed like a flower holding its seeds to itself when suddenly a wind comes along and—puff!—there's a seed here, and there's one, and there's one over there.

After this experience, George told God that he could send him to any mission field in the world. Passing the massive structure of the Halle Orphanages, he heard a child crying. He hurried on past the orphanage, but the child's lonely cry followed him down the alley. The thought of the cry lodged in his heart.

George truly wanted to follow God, but alas, he was in love. Ermegarde was the prettiest girl at the prayer meetings. She would tease George and make light of his new commitment. At one prayer meeting, George approached to kiss her.

"I love you, Ermegarde," he said.

"Are you serious?" she asked. "If so, I don't think I would fit in at all," referring to his desire to become a missionary.

George replied: "But you will learn to fit in."

"I don't want to learn," she said. "Missionaries are so—shabby and poor. I want nice clothes, furniture, a carriage. I just couldn't marry a missionary."

"But I am going to be a missionary. And I want to marry you."

"George, do be sensible!" said Ermegarde. "Why don't you think about teaching or law? They are both good professions."

"Are you asking me to give up my calling?" he asked.

"I am not asking. I am telling," she retorted. "You will have to choose, George."

George eventually discovered his mission. George chose God. In the years ahead, George Müeller would raise millions of dollars for his orphans, all by prayer and without a word of public solicitation. All through prayer.

And all because he saw one man living a genuine life before God. Just being faithful. Just being real. But being inspirational all along.

You can be a Brother Kayser to your children. Believe it. Inspire them with your godly example. Let them see you kneel to pray each day. Make sure that your faith in Christ is intact and that you practice what you preach. If you do, your children will be inspired by your example.[1]

Become a model of inspiration

The most inspirational experience that our children can know is a parent committed wholeheartedly to their

*F1 [1]Faith Coxe Bailey, George Müeller, *He Dared to Trust God For the Needs of Countless Orphans*, (Chicago: Moody Press, 1980)

welfare. And don't be discouraged! You can be the inspiration that your children need to become great in life. No matter what your past, no matter what your current lot in life, you can become an inspiration *if you will commit to the process.*

One father made that commitment and overcame incredible odds to inspire his children. Helen and Sam Walton grew up in the Depression era. They had four children—three boys and a girl. They made a conscious commitment to live in a small town and to work to promote "togetherness" in their family.

"One of our all-around inspirations for this type of family was the Robson family who were a successful, happy, prosperous family. I had fond memories of my childhood, yet it pains me to talk about one part of it. The simple truth is that my mother and dad were two of the most quarrelsome people who ever lived together. I loved them both dearly, and they were two wonderful individuals, but they were always at odds, and they really only stayed together because of Bud (my brother) and me. After we were grown, they split up and went their separate ways for a while."

Sam says that he was inspired to reverse the negatives he'd experienced as a kid and turn them into inspirational positives for his children. Despite the fact that he had had no parent to really inspire him to greatness, he committed to inspire his own kids to greatness. Then he set about doing just that.

"I was a scoutmaster. The three boys played football and did well. In fact, they each made the all-state team. I always tried to be home on Friday nights so that I would miss very few of their games."

Sam continues: "The boys threw paper routes. Alice was involved in horse shows at a very early age. Of course, we all went to church and Sunday school. I was a Sunday-school teacher.

"But after Wal-Mart was formed, we had less time with our kids. But through our combined efforts, our kids received your everyday heartland upbringing based on the same old bedrock values: belief in the importance of hard work, honesty, neighborliness, and thrift. As far as I am concerned, our values really took."

Sam Walton decided to be an inspiration to his children and then he set about doing it, much the same way he committed himself to becoming a successful businessman. Were his parenting efforts successful?

His son, Rob Walton, says that his father not only inspired all of his children to become successful adults, but he was just plain great to be around. Says Rob, "Dad went out of the way to spend time with us kids. And he was fun to be with."

Like Sam Walton, if you are ever going to inspire your children to greatness, you must decide and commit to being an inspiration for them. Simply put, you must be taking the necessary measures to make your life one that your children look at with enthusiastic admiration. Take heart, because this is something that Christians are called to do anyway. It is the essence of what Christ meant when he said to "let your light shine before men" (Matt. 5:16).

The single most important parenting characteristic for leading your child to greatness is for *you* to be the inspiration for the child and not what I call the "outside evil influencers" (see chapter 11). Some of these evil influencers will produce death, disease, and destruction for your child. Other influencers will change your child's course in life from where you intended it to be to avenues of unhappiness and disappointment.

The parent is fighting the major battle of parenting by

seeking to negate the world's evil influencers and by interceding as the child's inspiration.

Obviously, the other good influencers in society— over and above the parent—are much appreciated. But they are few. Let me assert here that you must demonstrate every virtue known to man or woman. A tall order, yes. You must guard against character weaknesses and protect yourself in the child's eyes. It is imperative that, as parents, we all cultivate, illustrate, and exhibit in our own personal lives virtues of bravery, honesty, love, creativity, spirituality, courageousness, fearlessness, sincerity, boldness, kindness, enterprise, courtesy, affection, charity, friendship, and devotion.

All parents should evaluate themselves on these virtues and determine where they are weak and strong, then strive to improve on the weak areas and enhance the strong ones. The more of these virtues that you can portray to your child, the more effective you will become as his or her inspiration in life. Inspired children want to perform at their best because they do not want to disappoint the ones they respect the most. That's inspiration. As a parent, my inspiration should be Christ. As a child, my inspiration should be my parents—and later in life, at time of salvation, it should be both Christ and my parents. Inspiration is a beautiful purpose to have in life.

4

Agreeing to Run with Them to the End

While one billion people watched via worldwide television, British sprinter Derek Redmond ran to qualify in the first four-hundred meter semifinal heat. As he bounded down the track, Derek heard a pop in his right leg—a pulled hamstring. Four years of agonizing training was seemingly all in vain. This was the Derek Redmond who had broken the British four-hundred-meter record at age nineteen in 1985 and again in 1987. He has held the European record ever since. In 1988 at the Seoul Olympics, Redmond was forced to drop out of his race when an Achilles injury flared up. As he and his father Jim traveled to Barcelona, they recalled that disappointing event in 1988 and made a pact about his upcoming race: No matter what, Derek would finish the race. Derek left the blocks in Barcelona in good form, but again, he felt the pain of his injured hamstring. Yet instead of staying down on the track, he waved off the medics who had come out to put him on a stretcher. Derek struggled to his feet. He began half walking and half hobbling down the track. In excruciating pain, crying big tears, he reached the top of the stretch, one hundred meters from the finish line.

High in the stands, unable to restrain his tears, his father, Jim, a butcher-machinery salesman from London, jumped to his feet. Jim raced as fast as he could down the stadium stairs, leaped the rail, resisted the pull of security guards, and dashed across the infield. His heart seemed to be beating a hundred miles an hour. The security guard hollered, "Come back, come back—you are not allowed on the field!" Jim was not going to break the pact he had made with Derek. He reached his son eighty meters from the finish line. Arm in arm, practically holding Derek up, they both finished the race together. Not even the Olympic officials had the heart to stop them. Derek was going to finish the race no matter what happened—the father and son had decreed it together!

Total commitment to the race

We can learn much from Derek and Jim's example. The first thing that they so clearly illustrate is that parents and their children must be totally committed to each other and to the child's goals if they are to realize greatness together in life. The most difficult, laborious, time-consuming, challenging, heart-breaking, and heart-warming job a person can have in life is to be a parent. No job, career cause, or vocation can even remotely compare in importance.

And we must stick with our kids to the end. We must help them finish the job of developing greatness. At times it may be an arduous task, yet it is one at which we can succeed if we know the principles to transmit to our kids.

To inspire your kids to greatness, it is essential that you teach them early in life and until they are out from under your control to *finish the task* that they started, just as Derek Redmond did. For you to be able to convince your kids to finish each project, you must finish each job you start. Your children are always observing your every action. They are looking for strengths and weaknesses in your character and will adopt them as characteristics in their lives. They do this voluntarily and/or involuntarily.

Your kids will feel very confident when they realize that you are with them either in spirit or actual participation in all of their activities. Instead of feeling lonely, they will gain assurance and strength by your presence. You can become friends, confidants, and buddies for your lifetime. They love it and are greatly inspired by it.

Do you recognize the names Mickey Mantle, George Brett, and Pistol Pete Maravich? They and many other athletes testify that they had fathers who commenced when they were young and continued as long as possible to inspire them to master their sport. Like Jim Redmond, these men made pacts—either spoken or unspoken— with their sons to run the race to the end ... together.

Begin early and continue late in *reinforcing* your child to consider all of the circumstances before he or she begins pursuing something in life; and be aware of your expectation for them to complete their respective en- deavors. The carry-over of this habit of running to the end in your kids' adult lives will be invaluable to them. It will prevent them from stopping tasks or assignments that would have produced great rewards and pleasures had they finished them. As adults many of us are familiar with what is known as the Endurance Curve, and we know that the greatest time of temptation to *stop* a project is right before the curve starts to go upward.

Being there for your child when the race gets tough

Jim Redmond was there for his child when Derek needed him most. Though in Derek's case it wasn't likely, still you can imagine that the young sprinter—feeling the pain that he was in and seeing the finish line still so far off—just might have thought of stopping his limp to the end of the race. After all, people were gawking at him. And he was all alone on that track in pain. But if there were any thoughts of quitting and lying down, they were surely dispelled when Jim came alongside his son.

Teaching your children to be committed to finishing the tasks they start is vital. But we don't leave them there. To help them break through that Endurance Curve, you must inspire them to finish their tasks.

Evander Holyfield was a five-foot, seven-inch senior from Fulton High School who weighed a meager 147 pounds. He grew up on the tough southeast side of Atlanta, yet at the age of eight, he promised himself that he would be the best at what he set out to do.

At his side in those early days was his mother. Through his adolescent years there were many temptations to stray from his goal and indulge in drugs and other trouble. He would later testify that it was Mama who helped keep him from straying off course. At age seventeen, the young man learned to conquer his fears and, as he would say later, "make fear work for you." And Mama was there to help.

Finally, after years of hard work and growth, Evander's mother was overjoyed as her son won the world heavyweight boxing championship from Buster Douglas. When he grants autographs, he signs his name and Philippians 4:13: "I can do everything through him who gives me strength."

The story doesn't stop there. Holyfield was later defeated by Riddick Bowe. After the defeat, who was there for him? Mama. She asked him a simple question: "Did you give it your best?" He responded affirmatively.

"Then you are still a champion," she said.

Evander Holyfield has always been a champion to his mother, Anna, and that has been one of his secrets to success. He could have had reasons for excusing himself from greatness. There was no dad in his home his entire childhood (when he was twenty-one, he met his father for the first time). Instead, Evander's mother inspired him to run to the end of the course he had set for himself. He finished the task.

If you're worried whether or not you can pull off the challenge of helping your kids run to the end, just look to Anna Holyfield. The greatest single inspiration you can be to your children comes simply *in being there for your children.*

When do you begin to inspire your kids to greatness? Just as early in life as possible. When do you stop inspiring your kids to greatness? The day you take your last breath here on earth. It is a beginning-to-end proposition. Your inspiration will continue long after your final departure from life. And remember, your inspiration will proceed from your kids to their kids. The good influences, like the bad influences, will continue on to the third and fourth generations in life. How remarkable it is to know that our efforts with our kids are so well-rewarded.

Finishing the race

Are you an Anna? Are you a Jim Redmond? Will you be there for your children at the beginning, at the middle, and at the end? Many of you reading this book are now living in your own "middle" age. By now, you may realize that the victory doesn't always go to the swift but to the persistent tortoise. By now you probably realize that your own greatness—or lack of it—will best and most fairly be judged at the end of your days on earth. On a smaller scale, any calling in your life, any project you take on, or any relationship you share can experience moments of greatness, only to collapse in the final analysis.

The point of this chapter has been to emphasize that you not only must teach and inspire your children to run to the end—to finish the race, as the apostle Paul said—but you also must commit to run to the end with them by being there for them emotionally, physically (if necessary), and spiritually until you die or they die first.

The odds are too great. And the pictures of greatness gone bad are too sad. For it is entirely possible to begin greatly and finish as a failure. Consider: He was the prototypical, consummate leader. He was tall, handsome, meek, and strong. He was obedient. He was considerate. He was energetic. He was a good leader. He was a victor, a winner. He was respected. And then things changed. . . . He was disobedient. He did wrong (which always leads to doing more wrong: We soon form a habit of doing wrong, and before we know it, it is our nature to do wrong). He continued to do wrong. He envied. He killed. He was killed. He died a failure. He was Saul, the failure.

The first king of Israel, considered the greatest of the great among his people, ended as the greatest failure of all biblical times. He was selected by God for greatness. He did not run to the end. Make the decision—the commitment—to teach your children to run to the end and then to run the course with them in whatever helpful and healthy ways you can.

5

Following the Equation for Greatness

When we say we will run with our children to the end, then we had better make sure we set the right course, too, lest all our running be in vain. A chief goal of parents should be to instill in their children's minds the equation—the pathway—for greatness. If it is not instilled into their heads and hearts, chances are they will never learn it. What is the pathway that leads to greatness? Here it is in the form of an equation:

THE EQUATION FOR GREATNESS

FRUGALITY + DISCIPLINE + SKILLS + HARD WORK + ETHICS + VALUES + BELIEFS

It may seem like a long equation. But life is long. Life is complex. Does the equation look like an uphill climb? Well wait until you get to the top! In the drama of your child's years, it will be so rewarding to see the precepts of this equation work their way out into greatness. In this chapter, we'll look at the bedrock of this equation or its foundational essentials: beliefs, values, and ethics. These are qualities that are more internal—more "head and heart"—in nature.

Start at the bottom with beliefs

The foundational bedrock for greatness is a proper system of beliefs; it is the element in the equation we'll probe the most. It is the basis for all decision making and choices in life. It is essential in the beginning. It is crucial at the end of one's life.

What a person believes and who a person believes will determine the routes that he or she will travel in life. At the base of the belief system that we must advocate to our children are the simple facts of the Gospel: that we can have eternal life because God the Father has forgiven us because of the death of his Son; that to reject this God and his Son's work leads to eternal damnation. Before going any further, I feel I must stress this point. It is imperative that we impress on our children that their journey in life can be interrupted by death at any moment. And the journey has a final destination of eternity. For our kids to make wise choices in life, they must be totally aware of these two options, which must not be regarded as opiates, figments of imagination, or old fairy-tales. They are real. They are unchanging. They are uncompromising. Every human being on earth will die and spend eternity either in heaven or hell.

If every goal in life were accomplished by your children and their final abode was eternal separation from God, it is clear that they would have totally missed the mark of greatness. This is the foundational belief. As parents we are obligated to instruct our children of this truism. Whether they believe or not, we have fulfilled our duty by making it known to them. Whether they believe now, later, or never, we proceed together traveling through life and employing all of the "how to's" to inspire our kids to greatness. We always have the hope of God's promises that they will believe someday. They must be taught that they must not base their beliefs on any mortal person's life but only on the Scriptures and the God that they reveal.

Are your children grounded in God's Word? Do they

have a solid, unshakable faith? Our kids fall short of greatness because they do not know the myriad and incredible promises of God designed to equip them to accomplish the impossible.

At the very core of this biblical illiteracy is a lack of commitment. There are enough Christian young people in America to turn the nation around in one month! Why are we having so little impact on our secular culture? "My people are destroyed from lack of knowledge," cries the prophet Hosea.

We must stir our Christian teens to a serious commitment to a serious belief system. We must teach our kids with enough finesse, excitement, and personal demonstration that they become excited and informed. This can be done through a variety of ways.

First, and very obviously, we can't expect them to develop Christian beliefs without incorporating "teaching times" into our weekly agenda. Our children must know not only what they believe but *why* they believe it.

Second, and most logically, we *illustrate* our belief system to our kids by our own lifestyles: the way we walk, treat our spouses, spend our time, and the personal priorities we live by. I am convinced we should use personal problems, errors, and addictions as a transparent form of teaching lessons to our kids. Simply put, let's not hide our hang-ups. Get honest and tell your children about your problems. Solicit their help. In the process, you will educate your son or daughter on the seriousness of every decision in life.

An essential ingredient of illustrating our belief system to our kids is displaying spiritual passion in our lives. Our beliefs are centered on God's timeless Word. However, without passion, these principles seem boring, restrictive, and unfulfilling. Passion in our lives as parents electrifies kids and persuades them that a belief system based on God is vital and even exciting for their own lives.

Shawn Bradley is a wonderful example of being enthusiastically committed to one's beliefs. The seven-foot, six-inch center at Brigham Young University was predicted to be the future Kareem Abdul-Jabbar. During his freshman year, he led the Cougars to a 21-13 record and an NCAA tournament berth. His first season alone he averaged 14.8 points, 7.7 rebounds, and 5.2 blocked shots a game.

Many said he could command a salary of $5 million. But the athletic star from Castle Dale, Utah, (population 1,962) interrupted his promising basketball career. Why? Shawn willingly volunteered for his two-year missionary requirement status as a Mormon. In Australia for nearly two years, he went door to door, without pay, teaching people the basic doctrines of the Church of Jesus Christ of Latter-Day Saints. And while Shawn has since entered the NBA, his commitment to his beliefs was and is admirable. This is the beginning of greatness.

Shawn Bradley was able to make this decision because of his beliefs. Another way of phrasing it is to say that Shawn had a standard. Our beliefs form our standard.

The primary definition of a standard is "a flag, banner, or ensign." It is a marker that commands and rallies the attention and allegiance of the troops. It stands as representative of a larger company of people or ideals.

In another sense, one's standard is formed from the summation of one's beliefs. Sometimes we say that people have high or low standards. What we really mean is that certain people have strong beliefs, which are set one upon the other until they form a high standard—a high banner or marker; or we mean that certain people have so few beliefs or so weak a system of beliefs that when those beliefs are set one upon the other they form a very low standard—or a very low banner or marker.

Everyone has a standard in life. Many people live by the Gold Standard; in other words, money is their standard; it is what they believe in and it is what they serve. But, of course, it is a faulty standard. It is serving created things rather than the Creator, as Paul mentions in Romans 1. God said that we cannot serve God and money. If you have not already done so, I encourage you to make your standard, your belief system, Jesus Christ. It is the best decision you could make for your children's future greatness.

Our kids will not achieve true greatness unless they, too, are deeply committed to their beliefs and ultimately to Jesus Christ as their standard bearer. It starts in our homes.

Establish values

On the foundation of our beliefs we then establish values. Like two layers of rock pressed together over thousands of years until the one seems almost inseparably joined with the other, so our beliefs and values are intensely intertwined. Values are the guiding principles our kids can live by. A value is the desirability or worth that a person ascribes to a certain belief—the estimation of the intrinsic, real, and inherent worth of a thing. If you value something highly, then it can usually be said that it is a part of your "value system." If you value something as insignificant, then it is not really one of your values at all.

A person's value system will determine the quality of his or her life. Does a person value money more than people? As we mentioned above, not if his or her belief system is based on the Bible, which says money has its place as a servant of people and God, not as a person's master. Does a person value self-promotion more than self-denial? Again, one would be hard-pressed to do so and still express sincere belief in the Scriptures.

Ultimately, values based on God's Word are traditional family values and are the opposite of the changing values of contemporary culture often based on a belief in relativism or humanistic philosophy. The second set of values operates on the premise, "If it feels good, do it." And if it is your desire to do something, then it is also your right, says contemporary culture.

But the basis of proper values is God's Word. It is our standard. It is the substance or sum total of our beliefs.

There is a sequence of logic that proceeds from the choosing of the right standard. It is as follows:

a. The Standard determines your Values.
b. The Values determine your Judgments.
c. The Judgments determine your Choices.
d. The Choices determine your Decisions.
e. The Decisions determine your Character.
f. The Character determines your greatness or failure in life.

You must encourage your children to embrace a proper value system based on God's Word. It must have their signature on it, as well as the family's signature. In a sense, every member of the family signs on a child's behavior and manner of thinking. Whenever the child is on his or her own, be it in school or playing or out on a date, the family is represented by that child's actions. Parents who are permissive and have little or no value system are apt to produce children with insecurity, hyperactivity, absence of boundaries, poor study habits, limited self-control, anxiety, lack of motivation, bad work habits, indiscretion, and a habit of going along with the group.

Parents with a traditional value system will work toward greatness and excellence by preparation through research and study; desiring to succeed; developing a real work ethic; having a passion to excel; knowing that success is measured at the end of a task, not the beginning or middle; agreeing that "comebacks" from temporary failures are a definite part of the process toward greatness; developing skills for success; ignoring the competition's rhetoric; observing one's "pain barrier," making necessary "gut checks," and knowing one's "anger zone"; smiling with a quiet humility through all of life's experiences; and loving the other person as Christ does.

On the one hand, if a good value system is in place, here are some things that won't occur around your house:

1. You won't "baby-sit" your teenagers through life;
2. You won't back-slap and back-stab other people in front of them;
3. You won't cover up for your children's loafing on a job;
4. You won't permit sulking and fretting;
5. You won't have different sets of rules for different family members;
6. You won't allow any family member to be a headache or a pain to the rest of the family.
7. You won't sweat your kids psychologically, but you will sweat them physically;
8. You won't dictatorially claim to have control of all areas of life.

On the other hand, if a good value system is in place, certain things are bound to happen:

1. Even if they don't actively participate in them, you will induce your children to have an interest in learning about many areas of life such as sports, music, art, languages, literature, drama, and science.
2. You will induce your children to participate actively in family covenants and to be aware of their value to protect the child (see chapter 15).
3. You will induce your child in his or her daily pursuits and activities by being an influencer, encourager, motivator, and inspirer.
4. You might teach your children how to cook. It's fun and challenging for them. My brothers and I know how to cook and are pretty good chefs. Our wives love it. My specialties are steak and chicken.
5. You will teach your child never to do those things that will cause them to surrender their freedom.
6. You will teach your child that the ultimate test of greatness in life is their relationship with God and that the second yardstick is the way they treat their fellow humans.

Family members don't singularly fail or singularly succeed. They rise or fall as a family unit. Each member of the family contributes, to some degree, to the success or failure of the other members.

Affix ethics

Ethics go hand in hand with a value and belief system. In the flow of progression just mentioned, ethics has to do with the judgments and choices we make that are based on our values and beliefs and that lead to our character or lack of it. Establishing a system of ethics is where the rubber meets the road in life for you and your children. Everyone is an ethicist just as everyone is a theologian. Everyone makes decisions and judgments concerning what he or she believes or doesn't believe about God; that's applying theology. In a similar sense, everyone makes decisions and judgments about how to act in life; that's using ethics.

Ethics is the systemization of our values. Ethics deals with applying our beliefs and values to real, specific situations.

Do you recall that wonderful stuff called Play-Doh™ that you played with as a child? Now, remember those wonderful machines called Play-Doh™ factories? You would put the playdough inside the factory and press down on a lever that would squeeze the playdough out the other end in pretty shapes.

Pretend that playdough is made of a mixture of your beliefs and values (Actually, it is mostly salt, water, flour, and food coloring—but I won't stretch the analogy). The playdough factory is your system of ethics, or the human filter through which you run your beliefs and values. You put your playdough (beliefs and values) into your factory (system of ethics) and press (think) and out comes your decisions in life. End of analogy.

Ethics—as a practical philosophy of human conduct that emphasizes making right decisions over wrong decisions—can lead you different directions.

There are really two types of ethical systems: situational ethics and absolute ethics. Situational ethics is based on the supposition that everything is relative and that how we act in a given situation is morally subject to change. It may start either with a belief in a divine being or with a belief in little or nothing. But regardless of its initial beliefs, situational ethics works itself out in a relativistic way. To call upon the apostle Paul, this kind of ethics starts with the Creation and leaves out any real consideration of the Creator.

Let's flesh this out by continuing our example concerning serving God or money. But let's add to the facts the following scenario: A woman and her husband are young and ambitious with big plans. They hope to make a great deal of money and *eventually* have children. Nothing is necessarily wrong or unethical about this yet. God allows some people to make a considerable amount of money for his kingdom use. And smartly planning your family isn't bad. But all of a sudden a new factor is thrown into the equation: They must make an unforeseen decision, or the woman is unexpectedly pregnant.

Either consciously or unconsciously, they now must ask the following questions:

1. What do I believe? (What is my standard?)
2. What do I value?
3. What will I do?

They are doing ethics. They are applying their values and beliefs to a certain situation.

In this case, there could be two sets of answers.

The first scenario goes like this: (1) I believe in an absolute God; (2) I therefore value life more than money; (3) I therefore will have this child.

The second scenario goes like this: (1) I don't really have any strong beliefs except maybe that "if it feels good, do it"; (2) I therefore in this case value money and the pursuit of money more than life (more aptly put, I worship and serve the creature rather than the Creator); (3) I therefore will abort the child.

As Christians we use absolute ethics that are ultimately guided by an absolute standard, the Bible. It is our ultimate governing principle. It guides our ethics.

However, in much of the secular world, ethics are

based on individual situations. They start with the creature and never get to considering the Creator and what he wants. This really exalts man as the ultimate arbitrator of right and wrong, as opposed to the first pattern, which regards God as the declarer of right and wrong and Christians as his faithful followers. Christians should be aware of these facts. In some cases, our system of ethics will agree with the secular world's. In others, it absolutely will not.

We must not only teach our children to do what is ethically proper, but we must also teach them how to think and make decisions about the day-to-day matters of life. While there is a certain kind of thinking that is more scholastic and heady, the thinking I am largely referring to in this case is playground, day-to-day, life-in-the-grinder kind of thinking. This is the kind that you do on your feet. This kind of thinking can be seen as the way we work oit our ethics—or apply our ethics—on a day-to-day basis.

For instance, often in a parent's presence, children will act like robots in submission and compliance, but when they are on their own, unmonitored, children's behavior reflects their true pattern of thinking. How are your children thinking? How are mine? Let's teach them how to think.

The simple rules for teaching your children how to think have to do with teaching them the causes and effects of their thinking. The logic goes as follows: *Thinking Rule 1* is that there is always a cause for a thought. It is usually an attitude. An attitude, according to the *American Heritage Dictionary*, is "a state of mind or feeling with regard to some matter; [a] disposition." We can help establish many of our child's attitudes by good training and conditioning, but we must realize that some attitudes come and go and fluctuate for better or for worse with as little prompting as a change in the weather or a missed devotion time.

An attitude can be one of optimism or pessimism—an attitude of seeing good in a matter or seeing bad in a matter. Is the cup half empty or half full? When your children are asked to share a toy with another child, will they view this as a positive opportunity to strengthen a relationship or will they view it as a violation of their own turf? Their basic attitude will make a difference in the thinking they do.

On an older level this scenario might work out like this: Jimmy's friends are giving another teenager in their gym class a hard time because the boy can't dribble a basketball without hitting his toes first. Granted, it is a funny sight. But Jimmy immediately must do some thinking.

He draws up his value and belief system first. He filters it through his system of absolute ethics. All this tells him that it is not right to demean another one of God's children just because of a physical inadequacy. On the contrary, it is the right thing to do to come alongside such a person and lift him up! But from this point on, Jimmy's values and beliefs and ethics must deal with his attitude. Is his attitude one of seriousness about believing the Scriptures? Is his attitude one of seriously living by convictions? Or is it one of flippantly going along with the crowd? Based on his attitudes, Jimmy will either defend and help this clumsy boy or join the others in mocking him.

Attitudes can be whimsical or deep-seated. They may be affected by what we had or didn't have for breakfast. Or they may be instilled from constant modeling by parents. But we must teach our children to be sensitive to the attitudes they bring to any decision making or thinking process. "Son," we must ask, "what attitude is behind that thought you just had?" Think!

Thinking Rule 2 is that every action in response to a thought has a reactive effect. In other words, we think, keeping in mind any attitudes that might affect good decision making. *Then* we act, always keeping in mind and weighing the fact that any action we take will have a reactive effect; we must experience the consequences and the effects of our actions.

Many teenagers get tripped up at this point in the thinking process. For example, Johnny is out with some friends. Johnny has just had a spat with his parents and his attitude temporarily is one of defiance or self-pity. The guys say they want to buy a twelve-pack of beer, go cruising, and get trashed.

At this point, Johnny would be wise not to go along with this idea simply because it is wrong—against his ethical system. But even if he doesn't realize that, good down-to-earth thinking would prevent him from going along with this idea.

First of all, if Johnny applies Thinking Rule 1 he would probably see that he is only tempted to go along with the guys' idea because of his temporary bad attitude toward his parents. That should stop him.

But with teenagers, passions can run high, so it may not stop Johnny. For the sake of the example, let's say it doesn't. So at that point, Johnny's parents must hope that he remembers their teaching about applying Thinking Rule 2, which tells Johnny to consider the consequences of his actions.

If Johnny does this, he would see that it wouldn't be wise to go cruising and drinking with the guys based on the possible effects or consequences that doing so could yield. If Johnny were thinking right, he would see that drinking and driving could spell disaster. He or one of his friends could end up dead. He or one of his friends could end up with a criminal record.

At this point, we hope that Johnny would say, "No thanks, guys," and even discourage others from doing so as well.

In summary, good thinking simply means: (1) being aware of one's attitudes and developing consistent ones as much as possible with the help of proper training and education; (2) thinking before you act, measuring the consequences against the anticipated pleasure or pain. As you seek to inspire your children, teach them to think. It could not only induce greatness but prevent catastrophe.

On this whole matter of teaching your children a proper system of ethics (applying on a large scale their beliefs and values) and thinking (applying your ethics to a given situation), it is essential that both parents be united in their training, teaching, thinking, and educational process to the child. If there is division, it destroys the training process. The child becomes a manipulator. The child wins by a matter of division. If the child disagrees with one parent and rejects that parent's correction and runs to the other parent, the child succeeds in dividing them. While this may be frustrating and tension-building for the parents, they are not the ultimate losers; the child is. This is the most common mistake in teaching or training a child about how to think or act, as well as with disciplining a child: parents' displaying indecisiveness between themselves.

To avoid such a scenario there should be a meeting between the children and both parents with an *open discussion* about this matter of the parents' being united; parents should agree in the presence of the children that the children are not permitted to "play both ends against each other." Then there is no possible misunderstanding. And it should always be a matter of prayer by both parents to God to help them be loyal to their pledge of unity. Nothing will devastate a family more than parents who work against each other by allowing the children to divide them in their instruction and discipline. I promise you that all children will try to play one parent against the other. And they will use every method and skill they can muster to do so. Don't allow it to happen. Your children will respect you and love you for standing against such a possibility.

When we teach beliefs, values, and resulting ethics at home, we lay the bedrock for the practical outworkings of our children's success and eventual greatness in life. In the next chapter, we'll look at the more external, practical side of our equation for greatness.

6

Hard Work, Skills, and Discipline

Greatness is embodied in an ordinary person with an extraordinary commitment, determination, inspiration, discipline, and concentration. The great "notables" we read and hear about are all ordinary people. But they are ordinary people who are fixated on hard work, skills, and discipline. Let's continue to look at our equation for greatness. In the last chapter we looked at the bedrock of the equation: beliefs, values, and ethics. In this chapter, let's look at the superstructure.

Mix in hard work, skills, and discipline

Be aware that one of the most compelling areas of life is work and that children will copy a parent's own attitude toward work. This is fleshed out in the "Apt To" rule, which can apply to all areas of life but definitely to the area of work. It follows that:

1. If the parents work hard, the children are apt to.
2. If the parents gripe about work, the children are apt to.
3. If the parents criticize their employer, the children are apt to.
4. If the parents are a slave to work, the children will be apt to.

5. If the parents respect their work, the children are apt to.
6. If the parents work for the right purpose—to please God, their employer, and themselves—the children are apt to.
7. If the parents work to escape the responsibility of their family, the children are apt to.
8. If the parents change employment frequently, the children are apt to.
9. If the parents consider a job or vocation as a privilege to have, the children are apt to.
10. If the parents develop continual improvement in work skills like self-study, self-improvement, and research, the children are apt to.
11. If the parents honor their employers in order to bring glory and honor to the kingdom of God, their children are apt to.
12. If the parents endeavor to accomplish excellence in their jobs and to ignore the status quo, their children are apt to.

Do your children ever hear you talking about your work? If so, what do they hear you say? Do you speak of the joys of constructive labor and of meeting a challenge and of the privilege of being able to make a living? Or do you gripe and complain? Remember, if you do it, your child is apt to also!

We need to teach our children that it is *good* and a *privilege* to work. Yes, teaching our children work skills is a mighty task. But we can begin with teaching them at home to care for their toys, room, and table-setting, as well as encouraging them to aid Dad and Mom with their household jobs (they will love it and learn from it). We must also teach them how to cooperate among themselves to perform household jobs.

Beyond teaching them about work in the home, take your children to various work sites outside the home; show them examples of different types of work; help them discover the work niches in life that your children will most enjoy.

One way your children will discover the enjoyment of work is to hear the praise and applause of their parents. A child needs to feel personally proud of completing work. Say, "Yeah, yeah, for Jerry!" We all love praise. Likewise, none of us appreciate ridicule or condemnation. Those can kill your child's desire to work.

But more than teaching our children that it is good to work, we need to teach them that there is a good and a bad way to work. We don't want to work *dumb*. We want to work *smart*.

We can teach them to work smart by teaching them to organize their work and to first view a task as a whole and then break it down into parts. They need to learn to think ahead and look for related work they can perform simultaneously. We can teach them how to look for efficient shortcuts. We teach them that they then need to sequence their work: first things first, narrowing the distance, and so on. Beyond these larger principles of smart work, there are other basics like avoiding breakage and waste in the workplace and working neatly.

Do these matters sound obvious? How far down life's road did you have to travel before you mastered them? We can give our children a big head start. For instance, when did you learn how to earn money, save money, and give money?

And above all, teach your child empathy for those who don't have work and aren't able to earn, save, and give money. This is our duty as Christians.

Discipline

Hand in hand with learning to work hard comes learning discipline. And this starts with teaching our children personal discipline. After having spoken in over 3000 public schools, I know firsthand that the average student in America today has very few personal disciplines. In fact, many schools—because of their problems with drugs, violence, and dysfunctional families—have difficulty just passing students from one grade to another. It is not impossible, but it is very difficult, to have discipline without having the proper bedrock of beliefs, values, and ethics. It is very easy, however, to have good discipline if the proper foundation of beliefs, values, and ethics has been laid.

The first requirement for a child to have discipline is for the child to have a teacher, mentor, or parent whom he or she respects, believes in, and will accept instruction from. This doesn't happen unless the child feels comfortable with the adult and confident in the adult's company. And this doesn't happen without spending large quantities of time together. We'll discuss this further in chapters 7 and 8.

When a parent achieves mentoring and teaching status, he or she becomes the authority. The parent then needs to develop a systematic training regimen for the child. The systematic training of discipline includes the total mental, emotional, moral, spiritual, and physical powers of one's being. It is literally bringing it all under subjection and control. Do you recall Burgess Meredith and Sylvester Stallone? Stallone, playing Rocky Balboa, submitted himself totally to the training regimen set forth by Meredith. He developed discipline under Meredith's tutelage. And he won!

The discipline should have a clear-cut goal for performance. In Rocky's case, it was to win the world heavyweight championship. And there should be self-imposed punishments and rewards for one's disciplined performance and for one's lack of disciplined performance.

The discipline should never be beyond reasonable and prudent performance. One sure-fire way to kill your children's spirits is to expect more from them than they can reasonably achieve through discipline. Our demands must be within the parameters of wisdom. A parent that drives a child misfires on this point and usually expects more from a child than is reasonable.

Simply stated, to help your children set personal discipline, earn their respect by spending time with them and then become their mentor. Ascertain the goal to be accomplished. Establish a system for accomplishing that goal. Write it down. Let your child determine the rewards and punishments for achieving discipline or not achieving it. Proceed with the regimen. Help your children to desire to practice their disciplines the exact same way they desire to regularly eat, sleep, bathe, and even breathe.

Here is a key: Induce your children to discipline first and to pleasure later. Disciplines will usually hurt at first. They won't be pleasurable. Adults know that as well as anyone. But then disciplines become habits that eventually become expressions of accomplishment and confidence.

Great places to establish initial disciplines are with your children's study habits, television-viewing habits, and reading habits,. How many of us adults are still striving to nail down these three areas? But the most basic discipline of all is establishing a consistent devotional time of prayer and Bible reading each day. In my opinion, all other disciplines begin here. A teen that has set a regular devotion time each day can easily set other personal disciplines.

Why? Not only is the child licking one the hardest areas of discipline, he or she also is feeding his or her belief and value system, which will bolster desire for good disciplines.

Frugality

Somebody once asked billionaire philanthropist John D. Rockefeller how much money was enough. His reply, "Just a little bit more." He knew what frugality was all about. When in the hands of a thrifty and wise person, no amount of money is too much.

Today's philosophy is spend, spend, spend. A famous Las Vegas entertainer who made millions recently filed bankruptcy. He outspent himself. Who hasn't heard of the professional athletes who suddenly made tons of money only to have it run through their fingers like water?

Frugality is a rare commodity that our kids need to learn in today's world where Americans run up millions upon millions of dollars of credit-card debt.

Teach your child the real value of money by implementing the following rule, which John Wesley lived by two centuries ago. Strive to make all you can; save all you can; give all you can. If you make all you can but don't save, then you are foolish. If you make all you can and save all you can but don't give, then you are greedy. If you make all you can, save all you can, and give all you can, then you will reach toward greatness in life. The parent must set the example.

Giving to others

It is of no avail to work hard, make money, and then hoard it. We must teach our children that the two chief reasons for working hard are to glorify God in our mere act of work and to make money to be used to further God's kingdom. Our chief reason for working is not to make money for money's sake.

How sad it would be to watch a child climb the mountain of greatness, laying the proper foundation of beliefs, values, and ethics, and building the external superstructure of working hard, being disciplined, and even achieving frugality, only to see the child miss the mark of greatness by being stingy and hoarding his or her material or spiritual wealth when he or she was so close. But be encouraged! If indeed you lay the proper internal foundation of beliefs, values, and ethics—as we demonstrated during our earlier discussion of how to think and do ethics—your child will most certainly be a giver, not a hoarder. Let's raise a generation of givers!

7

Give Them Time and Activity

The equation for greatness that we just dealt with seems involved, doesn't it? But don't be overwhelmed. As I said before, you don't have to implement it overnight. And there are two keys to implementing the equation that I want to share with you now. As we discussed the equation in the last two chapters, did you notice that two matters kept cropping up in one form or another?

Time. The first key, which we'll deal with in the next two chapters, is learning how to make and spend quality time with your children.

Communication. The second key, which we'll deal with in chapters 9 and 10, is learning how to promote quality communication with your child.

The two are intertwined. You can't have quality communication unless you've made quality time for it. But likewise, it is nearly impossible to have quality time unless there is quality communication. True greatness is achieved over time and via good communication.

So let's take some time to talk about time.

Where does your time go?

As adults and parents, we generally have time to accomplish all of our purposes and goals in life. Each person has twenty-four hours per day. Very significant is how each person dedicates and spends those hours. It would probably amaze each of us if we were to make a journal at the end of each day, week, month, and year about how we had spent our time. If we would log our time as pilots log their time on an airplane, we would probably be shocked by how much—or rather, how little—time we spend with our children. In fact, in your children's lives, from birth to age eighteen, there are 157,248 hours available for you to invest and shape them. How much time have you utilized at this point in their life?

Check it out in your own family. Keep a daily record for a week and be surprised. I have included in Appendix 1 a sheet that you can use to chart your minutes. If you record your time, you might even be a little embarrassed. Or humiliated. Hopefully, it will at least give you an awareness of your time and how it is dedicated and spent—or wasted.

A few years ago I was amazed to see how little time I spent with God, my wife, and my children. I was embarrassed at how much time I spent in my ministry doing things that I paid other people to do for me.

Take the time test! Be aware of your lack of good time spent with good people on good projects. And with God!

Kid-liking time is active time

Time for your children is not enough. They want *activity* and time. To inspire your kids to greatness, to help them implement the equation for greatness, they need you to combine time with activity. Make it private, make it enjoyable, and make it productive. The kids will love it and never forget it; and they will be inspired to greatness.

The kid-liking type activities are not what the parents

want to do only when it is convenient for them. These kinds of activity are ones that the *children* want to do. Kids' activities are as important to them as your biggest vocational, recreational, and personal achievements are to you, the parents.

Young people are crying for inspirational time and activity with Dad and Mom. So many students I talk with moan to me about how their parents never have any time for them. They yearn for it. They also yearn for activity with their parent or parents *when no one else is present*. What the child wants is to be alone with his or her parent, or parents, when the occasion is special. Take particular note of the teenagers who have regular interaction with their parents. It creates an amazing fortification to their decision-making processes and to their abilities to relate to their peers.

Here is an example of how I personally try to make quality time with my children. My kids love to spend time alone with Christie and me. In these private times they open up and what fun we have!

Because I am itinerant ten months out of the year, I take each of my three children on separate trips. They love it! Jeremy went to Miami and Anchorage. Danielle watched me perform in a heated debate on the "Sally Jessy Raphael Show" in New York City. And we both got sick together in Orlando. Now Jenilee is eager for her opportunity.

These trips provide far more than sightseeing expeditions and ministry to audiences. I have had the most intimate conversations with my kids on these excursions. We have actually become great friends and have learned to have so much fun together. Perhaps best of all, I truly feel that I know Danielle, Jeremy, and Jenilee. I am glad God woke me up five years ago when the most important thing to me seemed to be only "ministry." If need be, now I let the phone calls wait and the correspondence stack up.

The TV bandit

Today parents are spending little time with their children and even the little that parents spend is often without meaning, without content, negative, and with some person other than their child as the center of attention. The greatest example or proof of this statement is television. The family that is watching television is generally not communicating; the activity is by others; and the center of attention is the characters on the screen. This is not spending time together! At least not in the sense that will serve any constructive purpose for inspiration. Obviously, the child could experience this kind of activity alone, even if the program's content was worthwhile.

I have often been asked if I think families should have a television in their home. My answer is a plain, simple, but qualified "Yes, but it must be controlled with regard to time and substance." I believe that the television should not be turned on by any of the family members during controlled times of learning, recreation, chores, family communication, meals, or worship. These times should be controlled, and the television should not be allowed to invade. I believe that the rules should apply to both the children and the parents. The rules should be discussed, agreed upon, recorded, posted, and monitored.

Don't let television rob your family of good, constructive, enjoyable, and meaningful togetherness, learning, communication, recreation, and worship.

It is wrong for the parent to let the television destroy the child's ambition, values, or ethics. For a parent not to control the substance of the programs that the child is allowed to view is to give the child an open invitation to participate in filth (see chapter 11). Certain types of television programs are totally contrary to the proper family values that should be adopted by the parent and child. Don't let the child be sapped of his or her energy, ambition, or values. Television is one of the greatest threats to parents' ability to inspire their children to greatness.

Those hard personal encounters

Another example of a family's spending time together but without constructive consequence is when the family is engaged in a heated discussion or argument. Confrontations of this type can only negatively motivate a child. They can devastate a child's psyche. A simple rule to employ in these matters is for only the principal family members involved in the argument to be allowed to remain in the conversation or discussion. And there must be no onlookers. This is particularly true in times of reprimand and discipline. Other examples of when only the family principals should be involved in heated discussion are when the subject is either private or one of a modest nature.

When I say "family principals," I mean a mother and father, a mother and daughter, a father and son, a mother and son, and so forth. The point being that if the principals involved can resolve their issue, then others need not be involved.

To make the event private is to convey to the child that he or she is important and is worthy of the parent's time. To make the time and activity one of a personal nature is to convey that the child is not only worthy but special and therefore deserving of a special event with you! When all of this happens, it is indeed an *event*. It will be remembered by the child and will invariably serve as an inherited tradition for the child when he or she grows into an adult and can, then, experience the tradition with his or her own children.

Making family traditions

The legacy of an inspirational event in the life of a family is what makes family tradition so valuable and longlasting. For a person to say, "My dad did that, and his dad did that, and I will do that, and hopefully my son and his son will do that," is the glue that holds family traditions together and perpetuates inspirational learning and training. I know a young man who thought he liked to hunt but, by age thirty, realized more and more that hunting was not what he really liked. He would go out after ducks and come back victorious. But the joy wasn't as great as it seemed it should be.

Then the young man realized there was one missing ingredient on his hunting trips. His father! Since he was five, hunting had been the young man's special time with his father, who traveled as a salesman during the week. Often on the weekends, the son could count on at least one thing: He and his dad would go hunting, and they would be away and alone and *one-on-one*. No one would be there to disturb them. No one would be there to rob the son of this special time with his father. In the freezing rain or misty fog of a morning, watching the duck decoys bob up and down and waiting for a chance to call a big mallard in for a shot, the twosome would talk about life in a one-on-one way that they didn't usually get to do over the dinner table. And the son always felt a renewed kinship with his father after such trips.

Guess what? Now that young man wants to take his

boy hunting when his son gets old enough. And he knows the real reason why. He could buy a duck in the grocery store, but in his estimation there is no finer place where he could create better quality time with his son than in the woods.

This is just one example of creating quality time and activity that your children will love, cherish, and perpetuate as a tradition. The activity will increase in importance and educational potential because of the repetition of the event. This allows for so much joy because of the anticipation of the event as well as the experience of the event. The repetition of the event is the proof of the reality of the event. For a child to go the first time to a place and time of happiness and inspiration is construed as accidental, but to have the event repeated is to convince the child that "I am important; I am loved; I am worthy of all of this time, activity, and expense."

Inspiring your kids to greatness with time and activity is dramatically opposed to the one act that will destroy a child, and that is rejection. The single greatest way to devastate a child is to reject him or her. And that is precisely what a parent does when he or she excludes the child from sharing good time and activity.

Time could stop

As stated previously, the most important belief we can instill in our kids is an acute awareness of time and its association with their well-being. We should treat every moment with our kids as precious and memorable. We must never let the sun go down when there is anger between family members. We must value every moment as if it could be the last moment together. Because it could be. I don't mean to be a prophet of doom, but simply to tell all the facts, even those that hit us cold and hard.

Memories are wonderful, and they often last forever. For those memories to be pleasant and the type we will want to recall, we must forever be alert to the fact that each of our expressions to our kids could end up being a memory that we must carry should our child depart from this life before us. Time is precious. Don't waste it. Our words must be precious. Don't spend them foolishly. Our children are precious.

Consider the story of Karen, who wrote the following in her diary.

> God, in the midst of my friends' problems and my problems I pray that I will hold this song, 'Lift Me Up to Higher Ground,' before me and that you will 'lift me up to higher ground.' Lord, help me not to get bogged down by the sea of homework, the sea of frustration, envy, or just trying to be cool.
>
> Lord, just help me (whatever the cost) to concentrate on staying in the city of light on dry land. Help me to keep my focus on you, and instead of taking examples of others, Lord, please be my example. God, thank you for listening and understanding my problems from this humble cry of help.
>
> Please help me to be listening for you. Help me to be able to see you in little, day-to-day things. I love you, Lord! You are my best friend! You're the ultimate!
>
> —Karen—
>
> P.S. I hope you don't mind if I talk to you like you're my best friend. Thanks for being ultimately cool, God! Please help me and let me follow your example.
>
> P.P.S. I'll see you soon in glory!

Strangely this was the second-from-last diary entry of fourteen-year-old Karen Kayser. A vivacious girl who had

had no harsh words the week before with her three sisters Kathy, Kristine, and Karyl. She was in absolute harmony with her parents John and Marilyn. Teachers Joanne and Gord Robideau voted Karen as the one girl in their class they most desired to be their daughter.

This is someone we'd all like to spend time with.

Far from being homely, she was a charming girl with blonde hair that cascaded down past her petite shoulders. Her lips looked like little, perfect, circular pillows. And her eyes radiated. She was the type of young lady that any one of the guys would have wanted to be seen with.

She was the rare story of beauty and potential—all committed to Jesus Christ. As her diary so plainly revealed, Karen had an intimate walk with the Lord. Thursday, before her death on a Sunday night, her teacher Joanne honestly admitted to the ninth-grade class that she wanted a more consistent devotional time of one hour daily with God. The invitation was extended for any student who had the same hunger to meet her after class.

Only Karen showed up at 4:15 that afternoon. Unbeknownst to her, Joanne's ensuing words that day to Karen shortly before Karen left were to take on a strange double meaning, "You know," Joanne had told Karen, "we really don't have that much time left." She intended the comment to mean the school year's completion was coming soon.

As Karen left church on Sunday night with her three girlfriends, she was heard singing, "Soon and very soon, we are going to see the King." Moments later the accident happened. The Oldsmobile collided with a Hyundai and soared through the air, finally resting upside down in the ditch. Eight minutes after the crash, Marilyn discovered her daughter breathing slowly from her ears, nose, and mouth. Airlifted to a local hospital, three hours later Karen was dead. Father John's tribute to Karen retrieved memories from her earliest days:

— July 1975. A tremulous cry announcing Karen's birth, so poignant it squeezed her parents' heart with wonder and caused the tears to start.
— May 1976. Laughing, peek-a-boo from under the blanket, shocked surprise at first spoon of 7-Up.
— August 1986. Orange sun lighting up blonde hair, beauty in a child; the wonder of little arms around one's neck; the wonder . . . the wonder . . . first piano lesson . . . report cards. . . . Christmases . . . birthdays . . . holidays and always pleasure and pride in this growing girl.
— Edinburgh, Scotland, 1987. Instant Scottish accent, shopping, more shopping . . . this tiny girl . . . always full of fun, life, curiosity.
— May 1990. Clothes, makeup, hair spray and more hair spray . . . sleep-overs . . . always communicating. Weekly rearrangements of [her] own room, the living room, her sister's room, anybody's room. Open to the Lord . . . teaching four- and five-year-olds, concerned for friends.
— May 20, 1990. Horror of shattered cars and shattered bodies. Oh, how we loved her. Time.

As I talked with Joanne, Gord, and Karen's surviving friends, I was reminded again of the brevity of life. We are here today and gone tomorrow. But the Kaysers can now rest, although they do not know all the "whys." Why can they rest? Because they used their time together wisely and so when Karen died, they knew that their little girl was convinced of their love.

A few last words

If we are going to inspire our kids to greatness, we need to respect each day as though it might be our last with our sons or daughters. I mean this literally. I asked two seasoned parents who had lost a child what they would have done differently with their child had they been able to reverse time and bring them back.

Is the reply applicable to you?

1. I would have told him or her, "I love you just the way you are regardless of your frailties or blemishes."
2. I'd get my child to covenant with me to always be best friends; to forgive quickly and not hold grudges; and to be truthful with each other.
3. I'd tell my child, "There are a few areas in my life and your life that we should always try to improve on. You tell me your areas of weakness and I will tell you mine. Let's agree to work together to change them."
4. I would be certain I told my child about his or her long [eternal] life and where he or she would spend it. It is absolutely essential that we convey this truism to our children. We can't repeat it too often, that our long lives will only be one of two places: heaven or hell. The world is telling your children the opposite of this truth. We must begin early in life in our teaching.
5. I'd remind my child that if salvation has been experienced, because of both of our personal relationships with God, we will be together again.
6. I'd tell my child, "You did not select me to be your parent, and I did not select you to be my child. God placed us together. But if I had been able to make the selection, I would have chosen you instead of

any other kid, and I hope you would have chosen me."

Redeem the time. Spend time with your children. Spend quality time with your children. Tell them everything you think you'd want to say if you knew that tomorrow they would be gone. Agree to work together to change each other as, hand in hand, you shoot toward the target of greatness.

Once you've made the commitment to spend quality time with your children, you are more than halfway there. In the next chapter let's look at some effective ways you can better spend time with your children.

8

Laugh, Love, Learn, and Listen

There are, of course, myriad ways that you can create good times with your children. But I want to share one method with you that I enthusiastically endorse because it has worked for me.

How to create good times: Plan an L&L Event

Routinely and without interruption, plan L&L Events with your kids. The first L in L&L stands for LUNCH. It forms the basis for such events. Eating together can be so much fun and is easily arranged. The second L stands alternately for LAUGH, LEARN, LOVE, LISTEN, LABOR, LIBRARY, LITTLE LEAGUE, and so on. Can you think of more?

I include lunch with each event because *kids like to eat.* They do like food. They like restaurants, family cookouts, picnics, and all types of places for food. To tell a kid, "Let's do lunch," is like saying, "You are a special, important person in my life." It inspires a kid beyond your wildest imagination. And it begins with food.

The number of children in your family will determine the frequency of your L&L Events. If you only have one or two children, the L&L Events can be weekly. If there are more than two children, the events can be biweekly. The L&L Event must be one of time and activity. Young people love activity. They are bundles of energy. This is evidenced when they are newly born. Their body movements are almost continuous when they are awake. This energetic activity continues through the stages of crawling and walking. The same endless supply of energy continues through the ages of one, two, and up to about age seven; then they seem to slow down because of life's diversions, which seem to occupy them. As mentioned above, the greatest diversion is the time-activity destroyer known as television. It zaps the child's energy, negates his or her ambition to adventure, and destroys desire for constructive activity. Let's look at some great ways to make a lunch with your child a learning adventure.

The lunch routine

L&L Event #1—*Lunch and Laugh.* How long has it been since you and your child had a barrel-of-laughs fun time together? Here's your chance. Go to a preselected place that provides comedy, humor, and a good time. Laugh with your child. I love to laugh with my kids! When I hear them giggling for joy, my heart overflows.

L&L Event #2—*Lunch and Learn.* Have lunch with the aim of teaching your child *one* very valuable principle or lesson. Plan it in advance. Be prepared and welcome their questions. In this event, the parent must be the information gatherer about the selected subject. An example of the subject may be sex, abortion, gangs, family, church, God, etc. The subject must be specific but not boring. The content of the discussion must be pointed but not "heavy." It must have a goal but not be inflexible; again, always combine pleasure with the event. Make it joyful.

Another way to Lunch and Learn is to make the very act of eating an experience to train your child in different ethnic cultures, including their food, styles, fashions, decorations, and so on. I suggest that if it is a Chinese

restaurant you go to, have your child get the encyclope-
dia and learn about China and discuss it with you at the
meal. Let the child do most of the talking. Your study
and preparation should be used to lead/guide the child's
discussion. Don't overlook the fact that the goal of the
event is to learn, to have pleasure, and to be private and
personal.

L&L Event #3—*Lunch and Love*. Have lunch with
your child and together focus on the needs of someone
else. Together show your love to someone in the
hospital, a nursing home, or a person otherwise in need
of attention. If there is one thing typical of our youth
today, it is self-centeredness. They get everything mate-
rially and all that money can buy. Much of this teaches
them to be selfish and uncaring for other persons. We
must teach our children that true greatness—as mentioned in chapters 1 and 2 when we discussed having a
giving spirit—is not measured by what we have but by
what we give. Witness the famous and great widow who
gave her mite to Christ. Her greatness was defined by her
giving spirit.

This is contrary to our narcissistic society; therefore,
we will have to inspire our kids to *agape* love of other
persons, particularly those in need. Failure in life can be
noted by one's greed and selfishness. Help your child to
avoid that pitfall by inspiring your child with *your* love
for mankind and by displaying *your* sacrificial care and
giving. Of the three great inspirers in life—faith, hope,
and love—the greatest of these inspirers is *agape* love.

L&L Event #4—*Lunch and Listen*. Have lunch and
simply listen to your children. Let them talk about
anything important to them. Ask them about school,
friends, boyfriends, girlfriends, interests, goals, and any
problems. Be a good listener.

In this event, the parent should be totally relaxed,

quiet, and attentive. Eventually the child will open up and talk. Advise the child beforehand about what the goal of the event is and then don't discuss it immediately before the event. Take advantage of the surprise, spontaneity, and seriousness of the matter. Encourage the child that he or she should "make the calls" today about what is discussed. It is his or her time to "bring an issue to the table." It will be treated confidentially, with no reprisal, and every effort will be made to provide an answer in love and respect.

L&L Event # 5—*Lunch and Labor*. Have lunch and go to work together for someone else, a widow, a single parent, your church, or anyone in need. Have this project planned out, but *do something together for someone*. Teach your child how to labor, as mentioned in chapter 6, where we discussed hard work. Help him or her to experience the emotional and spiritual rewards of helping someone else. If you inspire your kids to greatness through a Lunch and Labor Event, it can actually inspire others to greatness by offering them help. Only God knows how a single act of kindness will multiply itself into other acts of kindness. God knows, rewards, and blesses all acts of kindness. Inspire your child to provide blessings for others, because this will bless God, and then God will bless your child. This is the "Cycle of Blessings."

L&L Event #6—*Lunch and Library*. Have lunch, then visit the library for a specific length of time to explore or learn or research something together. One of the greatest resources for inspiration to greatness is the library. It is a whole world of knowledge and wisdom. It will let your child experience mind adventures that are beyond your imagination.

The library is the source of knowledge. The Bible is the source of wisdom. Teach your child the difference.

But teach your child to explore the library. Adults should also realize that if they have questions regarding specific knowledge, they may call the specific department of the library. No one needs to be without true, sought-after knowledge. Library science can also be taught by the parent to the child as a means to inspire/equip the child to greatness.

L&L Event #7—*Lunch and Little League*. Have a lunch that is centered around an athletic event. Become a coach, buy season tickets to the professional baseball, football, or hockey games in your city and make it an event with your kid instead of your business associate. Don't waste your time with adults. Enjoy time with your kids and at the same time inspire them to happiness and greatness.

Sports is a great life event from which to learn. So are the arts and entertainment. All of our culture events should be taught to our children as a means by which our children can master communicating with others and just as a means for our children's pleasure. Just remember that every big-leaguer was once a Little-Leaguer in sports, the arts, and music. Each had a coach or coaches, who were their inspirers. Many of them were their own fathers. I enjoyed hearing Pistol Pete Maravich, the great LSU basketball star, tell me how his dad inspired him to greatness as his coach, mentor, and father. He loved his dad.

Making your L&Ls successful.

There are some basic criteria for making your L&L Events successful. First, for an L&L Event to be inspirationally successful, it must be *talked about repeatedly*. An example would be Dad saying, "Jimmy, this is Monday, but what are you and I going to do on Friday?";

or, "Hey, Jimmy, don't forget Friday, 4:00 P.M.!"; or, "Jimmy, what is our Friday event?'; or, "Hey, Jim, let's make some plans for Friday; you know, *our event!*"

Second, and similar to the first point, for the L&L Event to be inspirationally successful, it must be *eagerly looked forward to.* The anticipation of the event allows a person to share the joy of the event many times before actually experiencing it. This very matter will inspire the child to complete his or her projects, pursue his or her goals, and live life with joy and excitement. Life is not mundane because of the anticipation of the happy events such as a child's L&Ls.

Third, for the L&L Event to be inspirationally success-ful, it must be *specifically planned,* not accidental or maybe-ish. It should have an exact agenda. Here is the crucial test of any L&L Event you have with your children: Is the time and agenda exact? There is no compromising here. There are no "Let's make a deal" changes of the event. The child will measure the sincerity and commitment of the parent by his or her keeping their promises. Don't fail to measure up to your child in this regard. Don't let the distractions of life cause you to betray your child. Plan the event, plan your schedule, plan your time, and don't let anyone or anything interfere.

A recent TV commercial promoting a phone company told this story. A man had planned an event with his boy and promised him that they would do it, but then something came up at work that wouldn't allow him to leave the job site. The man was able, however, to use his trusty telephone to call his son and adapt their plans. At first the boy was saddened when he heard that his father couldn't come home from work and would have to change their plans. But then he was excited when he heard his father invite him to come hang out with him at his work site.

Well, while this is a nice example of flexibility and good intentions, I use it here to make another point. Don't change your L&L Events by the seat of your pants. Cherish them and follow through with them. This leads to the next point.

Fifth, for an L&L Event to be inspirationally successful, it must be *uncompromising in its intent*. The only "previously agreed" compromise would be an unavoidable emergency. I have known persons who would fly on an airplane all night or drive an extra three-hundred miles to keep their commitment to their children and their events. It must be prioritized above any last-minute schedule interruptions. To allow any interruption other than health, death, or emergency is simply conveying to your child that whatever or whoever interrupted you is more important to the parent than he or she is.

Sixth, for an L&L Event to be inspirationally successful, it must have *one parent with one child*. As we emphasized earlier, this is imperative. It is not private and personal unless there is one parent and one child. This can also break the yoke of a dominant parent over a meek child. I can't help but emphasize that a dominant mother can do devastating damage to a boy's personality; and a nonassertive father likewise can do damage to all of the children. There is a proper role of a respectful, gentle, assertive dad in a family relationship that inspires kids to greatness.

Seventh, for an L&L Event to be inspirationally successful, it must have *a variation of time, place, and type of conversation and activity*. This will convey to the child that the activity/event is not staged but is real. Also, the child will believe that the event is for his or her pleasure and learning and not for the purpose of programming him or her. You can use all of the specific L&L Events about to be listed, or you can be selective, depending on your tastes. As said before, maybe you can think of others. I recommend that all of them be incorporated in your routine.

Some people have tried each L&L Event and then eventually reduced them in number. Some have added new events. The real purpose is to accomplish two things:

1. Broaden the scope of a child's activities.
2. Balance a child's activities with events in life that help the child learn and that he or she will enjoy.

Watch what happens when your child realizes that he or she is important enough to have earned a routine appointment on your calendar. Your L&L Events will bond you as friends. Remember, this will be your chance to show that you care. Your chance to earn respect. A teen spells L-O-V-E differently than an adult does. Teens spell it: T-I-M-E and/or A-C-T-I-V-I-T-Y. If you combine time and activity, you will be on your way to inspiring your child to greatness.

9

Good Communication

The old expression that talk is cheap is grossly wrong when it comes to inspiring our kids to greatness. Talk is precious if it is the right talk and engaged in with the right spirit and manner. Talk is the strongest motivating force known to man. The apostle James spells out very clearly what the tongue can accomplish (either good or bad): "Likewise the tongue is a small part of the body, but it makes great boasts. Consider what a great forest is set on fire by a small spark. The tongue also is a fire, a world of evil among the parts of the body. It corrupts the whole person, sets the whole course of his life on fire, and is itself set on fire by hell" (James 3:5–6).

We'll look in this chapter at just how important this matter of good talk is. Then, in chapter 10, we'll study an effective model for improving your communication skills with your children.

Good talk to good people

It is always interesting how careful, poignant, and articulate we as parents are when we talk to a nonfamily member. We are generous with our words and kindness. We want to please the other person. We even patronize the other person. We go all-out to impress.

Why, then, are we so tight, constrained, and even selfish with our talk among our kids? They are our loved ones. They are gifts from God. Is it because they mirror some of our own personal characteristics that we don't like?

As previously discussed, making quality time is vital if we are to lead our children on the course toward greatness. But there can be no good time without good talk.

Commence immediately to talk—to communicate—with your kids in an inspirational way that will catapult them toward greatness. Notice the expressions on their faces the next time you talk to them and see if they aren't "on the edge" of being happy or unhappy according to your words. It even works with your dog! Change the inflection and tone of your voice as you give commands to your dog and watch its facial expressions. We owe it to our kids to talk to them more personally than we talk to dogs. Much more personally!

I wish I had a dollar for every time a parent has come to me (all over America) and said, "Jerry, you have got to talk to my kid. I can't get through to him."

You cannot inspire your children to greatness if you cannot effectively communicate with them. Every relationship in life revolves around our ability or inability to communicate. Simply spouting rules to our kids does not mean that we are communicating with them.

Communicate is a verb, an action word, and it means to "exchange information or opinions." Can you really communicate with your children? Remember, this isn't one-sided; it is an exchanging of ideas. Too much of our communication as parents is, "Sit down, be quiet, and listen to what I have to say."

In a southeastern city I sat with a dad and his son, Mitch. Mitch was angry and for good reason. His twin brother Mark was dead. One night Mark's rage exploded. He yelled from his bedroom to everyone else in the house, "I'll show you all!" Mitch spoke slowly as he shared this tragic story, tears christening his words.

"Jerry," he said, "from where I was in the kitchen, way down the hall, I knew that was it. I jumped to my feet and raced down the hall and started to turn the corner when Mark and I collided. The gun went off, a bullet drilled itself in the center of my brother's head. I watched his eyes roll back. And I just lay there while he bled all over my shirt and clothes. I knew he was dead."

Mitch's dad chimed in: "I just couldn't get through to him. Everytime I talked it was like he wasn't listening."

I thought about the story repeatedly. The dad was unable to make contact. Brother Mitch knew just from the tone of Mark's voice—even from all the way down the hall in the kitchen—that Mark was going to kill himself. Mitch tried to prevent it. The brothers could communicate, but the dad was oblivious to what was going on.

When your children are hurting, one of the great advantages of good communication is that the "door is open" for them to be willing to tell you about it. Isn't it sad that a parent is generally the last person to know when a son or daughter is hurting. Children tell their friends about their problems, or they will confide in a boyfriend or girlfriend.

Sometimes kids will even tell a teacher or a here-today-gone-tomorrow speaker like me, but they won't tell their parents—the people they live with every day. Why? Because the doors of communication are closed.

Develop strong communication skills so that your kids will talk anytime, about any subject. We must teach our children, "When you are hurting, ask for help." And we must be sensitive when they exhibit signs of a problem. Some kids can communicate quite openly when there is a problem; others hold it until sometimes, like Mark, they explode.

Empathetic talk to hurting children.

There are "Evidence Signs of Hurting." Whenever a teen withdraws, or exhibits marked behavioral changes, sleeplessness, inactivity, a noticeable change in personality, a sudden loss or gain of weight, signs of self-mutilation, violence, lying, or thievery, that teenager needs help. Any signs should be noted, monitored, and reacted to in a noncritical, nonalarmist manner. The parent should reach out to the child in a sincere, solution-oriented, team-togetherness way. At this moment in time, what the teen or child needs is a *friend*.

As a parent, try to become your child's best friend. You know what the qualities for best friends are. Try to cultivate those qualities in your life as a parent and be their best friend. You can do this with sincere, loving, and caring communication.

To premier, all-star center-fielder Ken Griffey, Jr., of the Seattle Mariners it superficially seemed as though he had it made. He had grown up in a well-to-do family. Baseball came as easily to him as chewing gum. He was picked first in the amateur draft. In professional baseball his is a renowned name. Certainly he never had any big problems. At least many thought so.

Nevertheless, by his own admission, in January 1988 he swallowed 277 aspirin and landed in intensive care at Providence Hospital in Mount Airy, Ohio. After his first season in the minors he came home. His late-night, live-it-up lifestyle caused major tension between him and his dad, former major-leaguer, Ken Griffey, Sr., who eventually told his son to move out or pay rent.

Confused, Griffey Jr., emptied a large bottle of aspirin

into his mouth. He says he has now resolved all the problems of those earlier days. What did he tell the general public about such an embarrassing experience in hopes that he might dissuade others from contemplating suicide? What got him through his ordeal?

The young star says it was heart-to-heart talks with his dad, Griffey, Sr. "The biggest change is that I learned my dad wasn't just trying to boss me around. He was trying to help me. I listen to him a lot more than I used to. I may not like it, but I do it."

Ken Griffey, Jr., discovered the real purpose of parenting, and that was that his dad wasn't just trying to boss him around. He was only trying to help him. If only every child could believe that his or her parent is not trying to be "Mr. Big-Man Boss" or "Mrs. Big-Woman Boss," but is only trying to help the child succeed in life, to be uninjured by life, and to stay out of trouble.

How do you convey this truth to your child? You begin by being a friend to your child, then by earning his or her respect, and by being sincere and pleasant in your communication. Though it is not easy for all of us parents to be "sweet" toward our children in our conduct and communication, it is certainly wise to do so.

Sweet talk to sweet people

So that a parent can evaluate himself or herself, I have developed a "Parent Sweetness Test," (see Appendix 2). It doesn't cost anything to be sweet. It is free. And it is so rewarding!

Become the sweetest parent in the world. Know your strengths and areas of weakness by scoring yourself. Take the Parent Sweetness Test. And then for real enlightenment, have your *child* score you. Afterward, compare your scores during an evening's discussion. In this age of everything seemingly working against the parent, it is imperative that we take advantage of every opportunity to improve our parenting. The Parent Sweetness Test will help do that for you.

Sweetness is nothing but an attitude. As we mentioned earlier during our discussion of the role that attitudes have in good thinking, attitudes are often predetermined before an event occurs. It is part of one's own personality to be sweet or sour. Sweetness is a wonderful attitude for the parent to display toward the child. As parents let's all strive toward being super-sweet in our contact with our children. They will love it, and we will love their reaction to our sweetness. They will be super-sweet right back to us. It is axiomatic. It is reciprocal.

Everyone likes to be around someone who has a sweet disposition. It sets life's stage for good, pleasant things. The people who are sweet just plain make the "taste of life" better and more palatable.

After all, sweetness is only an attitude that essentially tells the other person that you want to make his or her heart happy and that encourages him or her to pass on this sweetheart-happy attitude. Just consider how one parent, in his or her sweet attitude toward a child, can influence life all around the child. Conversely, just consider moments of anger or rage toward your child, and how it influences life all around your child. It drives the child away and makes the child go looking for another person of sweetness. It makes the child a sitting duck for anything that comes down the pike that has a measure of "Hey, I like you, let's be friends, let's go do _____." This is the very way that cults often appeal to youth.

Motivating talk to activate our children

Nothing is more absent in our American culture than good communication. Nothing does more damage to relationships than little or poor communication. Nothing inspires greatness more than good communication. Nothing will motivate a person to perform better than good, effective communication.

Consider a sporting team. The team performs poorly in the first half. They consistently make errors and evidence little drive or effort to contest the opponent. Their attention span is limited. They are almost lethargic. Their attitude, evidenced by their physical and mental expressions, is terrible. They are way behind in the score. The opponent is soundly defeating them.

They stop playing for halftime and go into the dressing room. And what happens? The coach communicates with them. In his communication, the coach uses every skill that he has ever known to reach the mind and soul of his team. He berates them. He scolds them. He shouts. He reviews their plays. He goes over the basics. He reminds them of their *future* absence if they continue their poor performance. He negatively motivates them. He positively motivates them. He communicates in every manner that he can recall. He is angry. He becomes quiet and subdued. He softens his voice. He stares at each player. He gets in front of each of them and chews on them. He is communicating.

Why does he do all of this? How can he show all of these emotions and skills in just twenty minutes? How can he be in control and out of control at the same time? How can he be so mean and yet so nice? How can he expend so much energy? It's all because he loves his players and he wants them to win. He is doing it for them. He wants them to play to the best of their abilities, skills, and talents. He wants them to concentrate, to be alert, and to be aware of the consequences of their actions.

He wants winners.

He wants to defeat the opponent.

He knows his team can win and he is going to see to it.

He communicates.

He covers every base of instruction and motivation.

What happens then? The twenty minutes is over. The coach is notified: two minutes. The team adjourns the meeting and goes back on the playing area. With all of this communication of facts, ideas, and information stored freshly in their minds, the players resume the game. They prevent the opponent from scoring. They themselves score. They come from behind. They see the score. They go ahead in the score. They win! They are the best team. They are happy. They smile. They do high-fives, hug, and pat each other. Why?

Because the coach communicated with them during the halftime break. He laid it on them. Why? Because he loved them and wanted them to win.

The same principle happens in the business world. The coach is the manager-leader. He prepares his employees. He trains them. He equips them. He explains all of the rules and regulations. The employees go out to perform. They lose the sale, don't make the quota, don't produce the product properly, don't perform adequately. They fail.

The manager brings them into a meeting and does the same thing the athletic coach does. They go back out to perform. They don't make the same mistakes. They apply their skills. They have been inspired by their manager. They win! They get the order, produce the product, and perform admirably. What happened? How did it change? The manager changed things by skillfu motivation and communication. He inspired them to greatness.

Let me emphasize what I said in chapter 3: We do not drive our children to greatness. We inspire them. With both the examples of the coach and business manager, the point is that they knew how to effectively communicate. We know as well that good communication comes from a good heart, and it will be evident to your child whether he or she is being driven or inspired.

The scenario for you and your child is very similar at times to that of a coach and his team or a manager and his business associates. The child is trained and educated, but the child fails. Why? Generally but not always, it is poor communication. The absolutely amazing aspect of communication is that it is free. It doesn't cost anything to talk to your child. It often doesn't even interrupt your activities to communicate. And it doesn't require a lot of time to communicate. You can say, "Hi," in a twinkling of the eye. You can say, "I love you," in less than one second. You can say, "Let's talk" in less time than that. We all regard our time as so valuable, but the time required to communicate is not demanding.

Forgiving talk to open up our children

So why don't we communicate? What is the answer to this common failure of people to communicate? Why don't spouses communicate? Why don't parents communicate with children? What prevents people who love each other from communicating? Why?

There are four basic excuses why. First, we don't want to be interrupted from what we are doing or concentrating on. Simply put, we are busy. What we are doing is too important. Or, we are relaxing. We don't want to be bothered. We want to be free to do what we want to do.

It is our right to be quiet, not talk, not listen, not pay attention to anyone else. We don't want to be interrupted.

Second, we don't want to communicate because we are slightly irritated. You have done something to disappoint me. You have hurt my feelings. I am going to get even with you. At this time, I really don't feel like communicating with you. Hopefully, if I don't talk to you, you will get the message that you shouldn't do the upsetting thing that you have been doing.

Third, we don't communicate with others because we fear what their response will be. We are afraid that a rebuttal, reaction, or response to our communication will be something we don't want to hear or to know. So to avoid the consequences and to quiet our fears, we clam up and don't talk. It is one of our chief escape mechanisms.

Finally, the fourth excuse is simply that we don't care enough to take the time and effort to communicate. By my quietness I am now saying to the other persons that they are not important to me. I don't like them. I don't love them. I reject them. I don't care about them or for them.

The first three excuses are a little bit understandable, they are based on selfishness, ignorance, and laziness and they mirror the character of the individual. They represent the personality of the person, and they are a form of self-centeredness, self-importance, and self-indulgence.

These first three excuses are really motivators in most all of the activities of any individual. They are not however, acceptable. They are undesirable. Instead of building up, they destroy. They are like a cancer eating away at a relationship. They evidence a total selfishness and a lack of wisdom and understanding about life.

But the fourth excuse, which essentially says from one person to another, "I don't like you"; "I don't love you"; "I reject you"—this fourth excuse is hateful and detestable. It destroys, kills, and crucifies another person. And when I think that this excuse often prevails in a family of birth-related, marriage-related, or adopted-related persons, I am totally appalled.

Consider: A husband and wife have a child and are thrilled and excited. They appreciate this tiny gift from God. The moments together are cherished. The expectations of the couple are satisfied beyond their wildest imagination. This child is all theirs and no one else has any claim over him or her! What a wonderful moment in their lives. And how they communicate with this child who can't even respond. They *ooh* and *ahh* and make all sorts of strange efforts to break through with their child into the realm of communication. They go on and on communicating.

Or consider a man and woman who see each other and are desperately attracted. They would walk through fire to be with each other. They talk about everything under the sun. They hang on each spoken word from the other. They laugh at stories that aren't funny. And they carefully, consistently measure each word before it is spoken. Each knows the answer and response before each spoken word. They go on and on communicating.

What happens between the time of birth, adoption, marriage, and a few years later? Simply stated, what happens often in both of the scenarios just mentioned and others similar to them is very similar to what happened with the athletic team. The persons in relationship make errors; they do bad things; they make mistakes; they perform badly; they fail; they are defeated; they disappoint.

All of this is regrettable but pretty normal for families

and loved ones today. We all do bad things or perform poorly or unwisely. We hurt one another. We say bad things. We act unlovely and unkindly. We are unwilling to change. Yes, we even act hatefully toward the one whom we previously loved, admired, protected, and cared for so much.

But what is sad is that as we err and fail and disappoint the other, often we also stop communicating. The channels either clog or deteriorate.

What clogs the channels of communication? What is the reason for poor communication?

The answer is plain and simple. It is as old as humankind. The answer will be the same in the future and in all cultures: *Unforgiveness!* It all boils down to unforgiveness. We have been hurt. We will not forgive or love the other person. We will not communicate with them even at the risk of jeopardizing our marriages, our families, our children. We will not forgive; we will get even.

It is because of this scenario that most of us fail to get on with inspiring our kids—or our spouses, for that matter—to greatness. We have been hurt, and we will not forgive, and we will not give them *agape!* Replace shouting, anger, and impatience with sincere, intelligent dialogue. Spoken words that are harsh, unkind, inconsiderate, impatient, angry, or belittling can never be taken back. How much we all regret the unkind, unloving, and hurtful words we have said to our loved ones. No, you can't retrieve them. But you can ask the other person's forgiveness. Remember that forgiveness precedes good communication. *It is equally important for the child to forgive the parent for mistakes as it is for the parent to forgive the child.* Many kids have been crushed by a parent's thoughtless words in a moment of unrestrained rage. Conversely, words wisely chosen can inspire children on to do far greater things in life than either they or their parents imagined possible. "A word aptly spoken is like apples of gold in settings of silver" (Prov. 25:11).

Before you employ the basic, simple rules of communication set forth in the next chapter, you must set the stage with each child whom you want to inspire to greatness by first forgiving him or her of all past deeds and misdeeds and by loving each child with unconditional love (see chapter 14).

After that stage of forgiveness and love has been established, then you are ready to move on to applying the techniques set forth in the next chapter. If the stage is right, the following formula for communicating with your kids can be a real winner.

10

Tell, Explain, Demonstrate, Inspire, and Listen

By now we should all be agreed that to inspire our kids to greatness, we must be effective communicators. Use the TEDIL rule to lead your child to greatness.

TEDIL is the acronym for Tell, Explain, Demonstrate, Inspire, and Listen.

The TEDIL rule is simple and easily understood by parents. When practiced, it shows that you care enough for your child to take the time to properly and adequately communicate with him or her. It is really saying, "I will thoroughly convey my message to yo, so there will be no room for misunderstanding. I want to inspire you to greatness, therefore the sky is the limit with regard to the amount of effort I will put forth and the amount of concern I will demonstrate to get you to believe me and trust my judgment."

Let's unfold this simple but effective concept of communicating.

Tell

Tell your children in plain, simple, and concise terms what you mean. Talk to them in a manner that is pleasant, kind, considerate, mild, tender, loving, and sincere. Often we talk, but our children never really hear what is said; or at least they don't hear what was meant to be said.

How many times after you have heard a speech or a sermon have you asked yourself, "What did he say?"; or "What did he mean?" Or, haven't we all listened to the newsmen tell us on TV what the President or some other speaker said or meant in his or her speech? If we can't understand these communicators (presidents, preachers, politicians, and so forth), think how difficult it is for our kids to know what we are saying when we generally spew out the words in haste or anger.

Explain

As you tell your child what to do, explain to him or her exactly what you mean. Especially in those areas of possible misunderstanding, explain things simply.

Explaining your message should involve two methods.

One is *repetition*. Repeat slowly and clearly your instruction-communication. Then ask questions: "Do you understand? Do you know the limits? Do you know the conditions?" 'Say: "Let's avoid a confrontation by my properly explaining the message, and by your properly understanding the message. I will repeat. You may ask questions. I will ask questions. Let's get the whole matter down pat so as to avoid any problems."

You must, as a parent, realize that your children will test this system of communication. We parents, as children, did the very same thing when our parents tried to communicate with us.

Demonstrate

After you tell and explain, demonstrate what you mean with options, movement, pictures, outlines, diagrams, and any other way that will add clarity. This type of communication is essential. It will clarify your positions. It will provide answers in case of unexpected problems. It adds to your child's belief that you care enough to inform him or her of potential conditions. It educates and trains. It shows completeness. And it erases possibilities for misunderstandings. It is a great teaching method for your child in his or her own personal communication to others. Demonstrate your inspiration-communication for your child's future greatness.

Inspire

Most important, as we discussed in chapter 3, inspire your child to act, perform, complete, fulfill, achieve, function, or execute every assignment or challenge that is before him or her.

Specific to this model, if you are communicating to your children through adequately telling, through properly explaining, and through definitively demonstrating, it follows that that will lead in most cases to your inspiring them to receive your communication. In a sense, this element of our model is contingent on the kind of life you have already lived up to this specific moment of communication. If you are living right, then your children will be inspired to really hear your specific communications to them. They can see it in your eyes. They can feel it in your presence. They know that what you are telling, explaining, and demonstrating to them is worth listening to. And that brings us to our next step.

Listen

Listen to your children's response, and you may need to repeat one or more of the steps already mentioned. As parents, we talk *to* our kids and we talk *at* them, but we often are not really listening to them. So much of effective communication is *listening*. The first requirement for being a good inspirational communicator is to be a good listener. Listen to your children. They have things to say that are important to them. *Don't talk; listen!* Your child will tell you things you need to know. By listening, you can discover his or her entire personality! Inspire by listening.

Review each one of these communication techniques. The most helpful way to recall them easily is by the acronym, TEDIL. Not only will the TEDIL rule transfer information, it will set the stage for parents and kids to have an overall pleasant and happy relationship. You will be able to avoid many of the potential problems and conflicts and create an atmosphere of family love and respect. A parent can demonstrate in action his or her esteem for the child by TEDIL communication.

Communicate by encouraging

In a study by one of the top ten universities, 2000 students in athletic activities were asked what they liked the most in their athletic activities. The number one "like" was, surprisingly, not "winning." Top on the list was "the positive interaction, affirmation, and encouragement of the coaches." The winning or losing is temporary and fleeting. The attitude and conduct is permanent and enduring.

In the game of life the most significant coaches are one's parents. As parents, we need to:

1. Interact on a same age level when it comes to understanding the child and on an adult level when it comes to conduct, example, and action. Never embarrass your child by inappropriately trying to act like a kid. Joe

Gibbs, the former NFL Washington Redskin coach, by his demeanor on and off the football field, never embarrassed his own kids or his players. I am confident that Coach Gibbs was always conscious of his inspirational influence on his kids by how he conducted himself on the sidelines of the football field and in the public's eye.

2. Determine to communicate positively, not to belittle, or to degrade. On this note, the parent needs to approach the subject of the child's character weaknesses (or sin) by acknowledging that the parent also has weaknesses (or sin). The parent and child need to discuss these matters frankly, agree upon them, and make attempts to provide solutions for them. The only character example worthy for comparison by our child is our Lord Jesus Christ. He is worth real discussion with our children.

The very worst approach to this subject would be for the parent to state or imply that the he or she has no weaknesses or sin, and that the child's weaknesses (or sin) are extensive and repugnant. We all have sin in our life. We are weak. We hurt others. We are insensitive to others. We are self-centered and selfish. We are preoccupied with ourselves and our own needs and are uncaring about anyone else's problems. We don't have time for them, nor are we really interested in them. We want bigger barns, bigger bank accounts, and bigger toys.

But when we know just who we are—when we properly assess ourselves as parents—then we are ready to share that information with our children and we set the stage for real communication and real inspiration. We become real to our children; they become real to us. The plastic phoniness has disappeared, and we are now ready to talk. Compare this method of communication with some supercilious, haughty parent who degrades his child about his sin to the point of no return and utter defeat, with no desire to change or improve.

Avoid showing disdain for your child when he or she is in sin, and only show disdain for the sin. Our words, our facial expressions, our manners, and our attitudes can destroy our children or inspire them. Take note of the very next contact with your child and see how radically you can employ this information and methodology. And climax the episode by saying to your child, "I love you." Just when he or she is expecting the verbal tongue-lashing, say to him or her, "I love you."

Be wise: Select the weaknesses of your child and yourself one at a time, not all at once. Do not overwhelm your child by exposing all of his weaknesses (sins) at one time. Could you handle that? Space them at times when the "communication air" is not heated with argument. Likewise, space the assessing of your own weaknesses (sin) out in time. As previously noted, the L&L Events are excellent opportunities for discussions of these problem areas.

3. Be a constant encourager; continually build your children up, inspiring them to achieve greater goals. This is the opposite of degrading your child. This is lifting him or her up!

No one should encourage a child more than his own dad and mom. A child's spirit needs to be cheered. When we foster optimism within them, no challenge or goal will seem unattainable.

Why should it be the parent? Because no other individual has more opportunities to be an encourager. It begins when we first see our children in the morning and concludes at the end of the day when they go to bed. Our greeting and demeanor in the morning is the forecaster for what type of day the children are likely to leave. If the day begins with love, friendship, moral and spiritual support, and a genuine desire to help in whatever need our child may have, that child will be reinforced with great resolve no matter what confrontations, challenges, or activities the day may bring.

Conversely, if we greet our kids with growling, scolding, condemnation, and distrust, these detrimental incentives will set the tone for an inevitable bad day. The attitude that originates with the parent is generally transferred to the child. A teenager with a negative, destructive attitude is mirroring a parent. On the other hand, love, care, and friendship are also contagious.

4. Finally, display affection to your kids. Of the prisoners polled on death row, 90 percent report the absence of physical affection from their fathers as the primary cause of their failure in life. Give them a big hug! It will do you good, too!

11

Battling Cultural Influencers with Traditional Culture

Contemporary culture and attitudes will destroy our kids unless we inspire them to overcome to greatness. We parents have a basic instinct to protect our children from bad influences and potential harm. If we parents feel that we can accomplish this first, instinctual goal of just helping our children get through life without terrible scars, then and only then can we really begin the next goal of inspiring our children to greatness. The new pop culture disdains the old traditional culture with its traditional values and flaunts that fact by ignoring the latter altogether.

Our best defense against this deteriorating culture is a good offense. That is to say, if we really want to prevent our children from succumbing to a progressively evil culture, then the best thing we can do is to equip them with an understanding of traditional culture and values that will enable them to do battle with the enemy—not run from it.

Battling culture with traditional and family values

The first rule of war is, of course, know the enemy. In this regard, there are many aspects of life that culturally influence our children. The parent must be aware of all of these. In one recent magazine survey, the respondents reported that only 26 percent of those polled thought that parents have the most influence on their kids, which was a poor second to a 49 percent showing by television. The remaining 25 percent represented the other influences on the youth of our day. In other words, only one out of four kids are influenced mostly by their parents in their lives' activities. From this poll it is easy to see what is steering our culture in America for our young people.

You and I know that we have the keys to saving our modern culture. It is traditional culture and values as expressed in the Judeo-Christian tradition. Traditional family values stem directly and literally from the Holy Bible.

Nobel laureate in physics, Arno Penzias, recognized for the discovery that the universe was formed with a (supposed) "Big Bang," said science has its limits and beyond that limit there must be other ways of finding truth. Penzias says that the love and faith that have gone into Judaism make it an ideal vehicle for understanding truths that are beyond science. "It is a wonderful way of finding that missing piece of your life that would otherwise be an 'empty hole'."

What do Jewish parents transmit to their children (age thirteen) at the bar mitzvah? The answer:

1. History—where they came from
2. Morality principles of right and wrong
3. Enjoyment of life
4. Definition of self
5. Community
6. Family
7. Faith

Religion, or our relationship with God, forms a basis for us as parents to establish a set of absolutes and values to teach to our kids. Even pediatrician Benjamin Spock argued that children still need to be anchored through religion. Spock stated that children first worship their parents because they appear wise, powerful, and rich. At age five, children begin to absorb parents' values. In his opinion, having strong religious beliefs simplifies the whole matter of giving religious ideals to children. "It is powerfully moving. Idealism is preserved. The lack of this is one of the underlying causes of unhappiness, stress and violence."

My reference to Penzias or Spock is not an endorsement of their theories or teaching. It is only a recognition of their values teaching regarding God and religion.

The benefit of traditional culture and values

What does it mean to be traditional? Tradition is defined as the handing down of information, beliefs, and customs by word of mouth and example from one generation to another. Tradition is an inherited pattern of thought or action. Tradition is a cultural continuity of social attitudes. Christians' set of traditions is built on a rich heritage of centuries of ancestors who lived according to a belief in God's Word and the values that result from following God's Word. What does good tradition do for us? It:

1. Provides time-tested solutions for the present.
2. Measures damaging trends and helps avoid them.
3. Evaluates and prioritizes personal experiences.
4. Views history as a teacher.
5. Reflects truths and falsehoods of the culture.
6. Identifies normalcy and abnormalities, good and bad, moral and immoral.

7. Offers advice to prevent repetition of mistakes.
8. Scrutinizes change before rejecting or adopting it.
9. Evaluates truth only with truth, not opinions or fads.
10. Collects the experiences of many persons of similar beliefs.
11. Affords a continuity of relationships.
12. Helps mold our basic attitude.
13. Prevents naivete about life.
14. Serves as a preserver of basic truths.
15. Affords protection against evil.
16. Provides a strategy for living.
17. Justifies its own existence.

One of the fundamental purposes of tradition is to pass on and teach to each generation what is right and what is wrong. Further, it teaches how society will reward or punish right and wrong. Teaching our youth right and wrong certainly includes instruction that, in life:

1. One will be right part of the time.
2. One will be wrong part of the time.
3. No one will ever be perfect.
4. God will forgive.
5. Family will forgive and forget.

Bucking the pop trends

Currently leading all of the cultural influencers are the businessmen who are going to try to exploit any trend or event all they can for profit. If it is a new trendy style of music, clothes, food, movie, or whatever, the businessmen will explore the economics of it to turn it into a profit center.

In competitive America the entrepreneur stands by

with the capital and the strategy to take a trendy item and put it on the market to appeal to the lusts and desires of the public. This development can happen very rapidly.

The trends shaping our culture follow a predictable course. A trend begins with a new fad of music, dance, or ideas. It is picked up by the other related fields such as art, literature, and so forth. It then becomes a matter of fashion for design. The youth pick up on it and help it along.

The social elite include it in their fashions. The media hype it. The businessman starts mass producing it to the populace. Prime-time TV includes it in sitcoms. Talk shows exploit it—and the more bizarre the better. The toy manufacturers emulate it. The status quo is attracted to it and uses it. It has become a trend. Then, we begin again with a new idea for a new cultural trend, because once the status quo absorbs one trend, it is no longer provocative and has no appeal to any of the other cultural groups.

Society has never operated without cultural influences or culture reformers. Culture is as old as mankind because it represents the sum total of man's activities. And there has always been a cultural elite. Even in the Communist countries there was a cultural elite. However, today it is different for two reasons: vulgarity and violence. It makes no matter what area of society you consider, there now exists the potential for instantaneous actions of vulgarity or violence.

Therefore, we must train our children to recognize these cultural influencers and trends and to avoid them when they compromise our personal respect and decency or well-being. Every parent must ask himself or herself, "Will I be the cultural influencer of my child, or will it be one or more of the other cultural elite and the culture shapers?"

The cultural elite and the culture shapers want to reach and influence your child. Why?

1. Hurting people do it to express their pain and suffering.
2. Members of the various arts do it to influence our culture for recognition in their field (and for money).
3. The media does it to sell their network, for money.
4. The academic does it to establish a new thesis about life, for money.
5. The lawyer does it to represent his client, regardless of which side he is on, for money.
6. The businessman does it for money.
7. The politician does it for votes (for money).
8. The comedian does it for laughs (for money).
9. The movies do it to either motivate or reflect society (for money).
10. The publisher does it to sell newspapers, magazines, videos, or books (for money).
11. The social engineer does it to develop his new thesis to change society to conform to and to enhance his social and political outlook.
12. The social elite do it to read about themselves on the society page and columns.
13. The talk-show host does it to increase his rating (for money).

Consider the following as an incomplete list of those who are changing our culture every day. Consider how you can forewarn your children of these potentially dangerous cultural influencers and develop a family strategy to cope with them:

1. Music
2. Movies
3. Politicians
4. Academicians (Educators)
5. Artists
6. Writers, Authors, Editorialists
7. Publishers — print and video
8. Lawyers
9. Television
10. Advertising
11. Cable TV
12. Sports Violence
13. Sports Personalities
14. TV Evangelists
15. Gay Movement
16. So-called Intellectuals
17. Feminists
18. Cults
19. Fashion Designers
20. MTV Performers
21. Rock Performers
22. Cartoons (Simpsons)
23. Comedy
24. TV Satire (Saturday Night Live)
25. Talk Show Hosts
26. News Media
27. Gangs
28. Beer Commercials
29. Education for a Profit
30. Japanese Investments
31. Futurists
32. Critics
33. Social Engineers
34. Rappers

A sex-crazed culture

Our kids today are submerged in a cultural value system that attempts to eradicate their faith and pull them down. And one of the most effective tools of this culture is a perverse view of the godly gift of sex.

This is what you are up against: Provocative bombshell Madonna shoots 20,000 photos with Steven Meisel; 475 are printed; and her book *Sex* becomes a U.S. bestseller of 500,000 copies. It sold out in Britain and Australia. *Entertainment Weekly* summed up the book's features as follows:

1. Pictures of women in shaved heads and tattoos: 28
2. Nipple shots: 84
3. Detailed explanation of anal sex: 1
4. Photos with a finger or toe in someone's mouth: 3

5. Urine shots that recall Mapplethorpe: 3
6. Pierced body parts: 4
7. Men in dog collars: 9
8. Things that look like they hurt: 6
9. Penises shown: 1
10. Times God is mentioned: 3

It goes without saying that you can't win the war if you don't know the enemy and don't have the tools with which to fight the enemy. *There she is!* This war for our culture is the most important that most of us will ever fight. It is for the souls and lives of our children—and ourselves.

Demonstrating just how bold, arrogant, and trashy the culture changers can be, Madonna, in a blatant insult to every parent in America, has publicly stated: "I am going to change our society about the subject of sex." And the public is doing nothing about it. Talk about the boom of a "porn-again" movement. How sad. How far we have fallen that someone like Madonna would be lauded as artistic and a marketing genius.

The onslaught of sex is pervasive. We cannot hand out Bibles on public school campuses, but others can hand out condoms. The New York City school system distributed 100,000. Magic Johnson tragically contracted the AIDS virus and after his disclosure was heralded as a hero. *Newsweek's* periodic front cover features on AIDS recently approached the subject from a new angle. It blared: "AIDS Among Teens." Could this epidemic prompt us to a clarion call for abstinence and sex only within the confines of marriage—one man for one woman? Apparently not. A congressional report issued recently warned that HIV, the virus that causes AIDS, is "spreading unchecked among the nation's adolescents, regardless of where they live or their economic status."

Since the beginning of the epidemic, more than 5000 children and young adults have died of AIDS; it is now the sixth leading cause of death among fifteen- to twenty-four-year-olds. No one knows exactly how many teens are HIV-positive, but during the past three years, the cumulative number of thirteen- to fourteen-year-olds diagnosed with AIDS increased 77 percent. By the end of last 1991, AIDS cases in the aforementioned age group had been reported in almost every state and the District of Columbia. Nearly half of the afflicted teenagers come from just six places: New York, New Jersey, Texas, California, Florida, and Puerto Rico.

The homosexual revolution

When "a concerned father" from Ukiah, California, wrote Ann Landers, alarmed that his son's teacher was informing his class of five sexes in the human race: male, female, homosexual, bisexual, and asexual—he wanted her response. Geared to our decaying times, she responded, "There are only two sexes—male and female. Recent studies indicate that homosexuality, bisexuality, and asexuality are not the result of something that has gone wrong with the sex organs, but rather a biochemical-genetic alteration that no one has been able to explain."

I am deeply concerned about the "gay boom" among young people in our evangelical churches and colleges, who keep coming to me and others, wanting freedom. Recently, one young man, a youth group leader, came to me in tears after a meeting, begging for help. He had been covertly gay for years and even involved in bestiality! His parents, good church-goers, were oblivious to his desperate condition.

Homosexuality is not genetic; it is not born or bred. It

is a choice, often prompted when Dad and Mom do not connect with a young man or woman at the critical time regarding the vital issues of masculinity, femininity, sexuality, and God's standards.

The decline of Christian America

Slowly, America is ceasing to be a "Christian nation." Statistics regarding our religiosity reveal a new morality is sweeping the nation. Publisher Robert J. Dowling in the 62nd Anniversary issue of the *Hollywood Reporter* writes, "Entertainment, in fact, is a reflection of our society. Movies and music of the past reflected their 'today' yesterday in the same way they represent our today, today. If what we see in our entertainment causes us concern, we should look more toward the origins of the message and less to the messenger." Hollywood purveyors cannot abdicate their contribution to the sewage of material ingratiating itself to millions, young and old alike. Family values, wholesome values, are a fleeting item to our entertainment culture. Every parent should read *Hollywood vs. America* by Michael Medved. He has done his homework and documents how some media moguls are trying to take us to hell with them.

Gone are the days of *My Three Sons*, instead replaced by TV's number one show, *Roseanne*, with its newly introduced gay character. We must deflect these negative influences aimed at our kids.

Deflecting culture's negative influence

One method I have found to be effective in battling the prevailing culture is to talk openly with my children about what message certain TV shows, movies, and types of music are attempting to convey. As we discuss issues of excessive violence, raw sex, or sexual perversion, and a "no-absolutes" philosophy of entertainment, I am able to reinforce God's opinion that is revealed in his Word.

Furthermore, I have the opportunity to model for them. They are always interested in what movie Dad and Mom went to see. Every principle I share with them becomes null and void if it is not lived out in Christie's and my life before them.

The basis of all of our principles and convictions is a literal belief in God's Word, the Bible. We do not approach it with a pick-and-choose attitude. We accept its authority over all matters and have the sober responsibility to instill its principles into our children. And it then follows that our leader, our supreme model, is Jesus Christ. The more our children see Christ in us, the more they will be detoured from the vain, insincere philosophy of the world. Who will do something about this slippage in our culture? You can, first by standing against such moral slippage yourself. But perhaps the greatest contribution you could make is to reproduce yourself and your beliefs in your children. Let's make a generation of children who grow up to stem the tide of our deteriorating culture by standing for God and for traditional values. This would constitute true greatness in our children! This vision will never be accomplished, however, unless our children are as competitive as the next person's. That is what we will deal with in chapters 12 and 13. We'll address how we can encourage our children toward being properly competitive.

12

Making Them Competitive

Competition is the driving force that inspires men and women to greatness. It is a force that can be conquered. Never has there been more competition than in today's world. If we are going to inspire our kids to greatness, we are going to have to teach them to conquer competition. At the same time, they must learn to control their competitive activities and events. We must never impress on our kids that competition without controls and balance is the answer. An example of unrestrained competition is our political world, which is full of competitive compromises and failed promises. An example of unrestrained competition in the sporting world is out-of-control violence that far exceeds the rules. Witness ice hockey on television for a real insight into out-of-control sports violence. An example of unrestrained competition in our Christian world is beyond-acceptable limits of commercializing our various national ministries. An example of unrestrained personal competition is the abuse of alcohol and drugs to enhance performance.

The sky is the limit of uncontrolled, unrestrained competition. We see it all around us. And our kids really see it! It is little wonder that it scares them to the point that they want to drop out, not try, and just give up.

Your child's competition

Our competition is not limited to family, city, and nation. It is now international; and the trend is for it to supersede all rules of nationalism and head onward to the "new world order," unless we do something about it. Without a competitive spirit, our kids will not be able to exist, let alone succeed or aspire to greatness. =
Imagine this schedule. He or she:

1. Rises at about 6:30 A.M.
2. Has relentless pressure to get ahead.
3. Works a full day with his or her regular companions.
4. Studies an additional three hours in the evening.
5. Works a couple of hours at home.
6. Goes to bed at midnight.
7. Has an immediate goal of gaining admission to a prestigious university and a long-term goal of getting a good job with a good company.
8. Is constantly thinking and preparing for the future.
9. Struggles to succeed.
10. Participates in cram schools called "jukers."
11. Knows his or her society is based on a merit system.
12. Cannot take up after-school sports or hobbies. No time.
13. Has very little freedom from studying.

How old is this person? Incredibly, eleven years old! The Japanese educational system prides itself in producing achievers. A Japanese child must be in school between the ages of six and fifteen. Generally children enter formal schooling at age three or four. A stunning 94 percent of them finish high school.

Take note of the striking differences between Japan's regimen and our U.S. school system:

1. Japan's school year begins April 1 and ends in March the following year, approximately 240 days of education compared to our 180.
2. Classes are held for half a day on Saturdays.
3. Schools are plain in Japan. Compared with American standards, they are physically unattractive.
4. The Japan curriculum is so respected that a high-school diploma there can be said to be equivalent of a college degree in the U.S.
5. Homework is assigned to a first-grader, and by high school a student spends several hours a day on homework (65 percent Japanese compared to 24 percent by American students). =
6. Every Japanese student takes years of what is described as "moral education." A child studies behavior and relationships within the family and community. The child is carefully taught to persevere, possess sincerity, and show good cheer.
7. To be good is to be strong. The Japanese system encourages pushing oneself as hard as one can. There is extensive physical education, morning exercises, and then more specialized courses. There are few school "jocks." The purpose of athletics is not gaming or sport but to stretch the limit of physical endurance.

And where do Mom and Dad fit in? This is what is particularly notable. In this culture the parents are responsible for the educational competitiveness of the child. They work in direct unison with the faculty. The goal is to produce an intelligent student who has his or her future planned and who is prepared. This is serious business: How well a child does in the schoolroom is felt by Japanese to be the most important determinant of Japan's future place in the world.

Unlike our society where an unemployed mother is considered "just a housewife," Japanese mothers have been called "the best Jewish mothers in the world." Japanese mothers feel responsible for their children's future. The Confucian-based value system exalts motherhood more than wifehood.

The majority of Japanese mothers believe that their first responsibility is to their children.

The majority of Japanese mothers do not work outside of the home. From the very moment of conception, the Japanese mother wants to cement a bond with the child. This goal continues throughout childhood.

Obviously there are some problems with the intense educational pressure imposed on Japanese students. As in America, there is a significant youth suicide problem. Peer pressure is a second contributor to Japanese young people's committing suicide. Statistically, however, U.S. students exceed Japanese youth in completed suicides.

Vocations of desire and need

If our youth are going to compete with the likes of those previously described, inspiring our kids to greatness must include helping our children discover their "niche in life." In other words, we must help them discover their career choice. There are two common methods for making this discovery. One is to help them see what they desire or are most interested in pursuing as a life work. The other is to help them discover a need in life that they can help fill.

Simply remember: *desire and need!* When you and your child discover his or her area of desire, you can help your child research to uncover the various options for work that exist in that field. For instance, in the field of sports there are the areas of athlete, coach, sports psychologist, reporter, announcer, statistician, marketer and promoter, scouter, trainer, researcher, and so on. In other words, not everyone has to be the athlete. If the child desires to be an athlete but discovers that he or she can't compete in the upper echelon, then the parent will want to help him or her discover the related areas of sports other than being an athlete.

I was very interested in a school project my thirteen-year-old, Danielle, was doing while I was in the process of writing this chapter. All the pupils in her language arts class were required to do an "I Search" paper. Basically the kids had to come up with a question and then find the answers to it. Danielle has always had an interest in the medical field so she chose to research the question, Should I be a Doctor?.

One of the requirements for research on this paper was to ask two doctors a bundle of questions, basically gathering the positives and negatives of the occupation.

When Danielle started on this little journey, I wasn't sure if she would lose heart and adapt an attitude of, "Oh it's just too much trouble," or, "There is just too much of a price to pay to be a doctor"; but I must tell you, she refused to be discouraged by the negatives. I was impressed and proud of her tenacity and desire.

Discovering a need in life involves having the parent and child zero in on a field where there are voids of service but needs for service. An example might be that if your child likes the medical field but later discovers that he or she does not want to be a doctor, you can help the child discover an area in the field of medicine where there is a need, such as teaching medicine, pharmaceutical research, science, nursing, medical technology, dentistry, office management, hospital administration, and so on.

In other words, if medicine is his or her interest and there is a need for medical missionaries in the area of nursing, administration, research, science, or hospital work, help the child discover this area of choice. The key is to help your child narrow the overall field and then discover a specific area in the field.

Considering all the fields of endeavor, it is pitiful that a child can be with parents and family for eighteen years and go through elementary, middle, and high school and not know what he or she wants to pursue as a vocational career.

Compound this terrible "career condition" with the fact that many of our youth even go through college without still not really knowing what they want to pursue as their vocation. It is unreal to think that parents are so disinterested in their children and that our school systems are that inept in teaching and guiding our youth.

My wife and I have made a point of teaching our children to be specific about what they want to do in life. Whether it just be for the day, or the summer, or for life. Don't waver back and forth. We used to chuckle at our son Jeremy, who, ever since he was nine, talked every day about growing up to be an NFL quarterback and a pastor in the off-season.

Shortly thereafter, we got into quite a lengthy conversation with our kids about the specificity of their desires. We explained to them that God is waiting to do something great with their lives, but they needed to ask him in a specific way for a specific purpose. Little did we realize what an impact it would have on our son! He began starting his prayers with, "Dear God, please make me an NFL *first-string* quarterback and pastor in the off-season."

Jeremy came to the realization that being an NFL quarterback wasn't quite good enough. He had to become the *first-string* field general. When will parents take seriously their children and their career choices? Begin early. Make the discovery of career by desire and need. Explore every avenue. Have family discussions. Visit the library.

To inspire your kids to greatness, help them discover their niche in life by either discovering their desire and interest in life's vocations, or discovering a need in their lives that they can help fill in service to their fellow man. With God's help, our children can often find a vocation that both fills a need and meets their desires.

The deterrents to vocational greatness

There are two sure-fire deterrents to your children's achieving greatness through his vocation. The first sure-fire deterrent is to have them in areas of vocation that they are not even remotely interested in, which is like putting a square peg in a round hole. There is no fit. Teach your children to be leaders within their gifts. If they are sincerely interested in a desired field, and if there is a real need there, they will feel challenged to be the best and will pay the "pain price" to achieve their goals. The rewards will be important but not all-important.

Frequently the parent will, by design or by accident, look down at or degrade the child's chosen profession; that is the second sure-fire deterrent to greatness in life. A famous baseball manager once showed a terrible attitude toward his son who did not want to be an athlete but was interested in music. After several years of surface bitterness, the father said, "I finally grew up and accepted my son's choice and helped him pursue his vocation."

In the area of our children's chosen professions it takes a long time for some of us parents to grow up, get wise, and help our children prepare and proceed with *their* decisions in life, regarding jobs, marriage, friends, churches, and so on.

If your children exercise their desire to discover their career and to combine it with fulfilling a need in life, they then only have to exercise their God-given talents, abilities, and gifts. All children have them and they will surely mesh with their desired or need-filled career choice if they have made the right choice. God will empower their talents, abilities, and gifts, which he already has given them. We just need to help our children make the discovery.

Prepared reaction responses

To be competitive, also teach your child how to react to conditions that must be acted upon immediately. They will certainly need this skill no matter what vocation they finally enter. For that matter, they'll need it in their church, on the highway, or in the grocery store. We must lead them to establish "prepared reaction responses" to any potential predicament they may find themselves in. To make those right, instantaneous decisions where the reaction time is so brief is often the difference between victory in one's life or heartache. In many ways this has to do with the two rules of thinking that we discussed in chapter 5.

In professional baseball a batter knows that the pitcher can't throw many different types of balls. In fact, from the time the baseball leaves the major-league pitcher's hand the batter has only two-tenths of a second to decide if he is going to swing at it or take the ball. And, as the home-run records reveal, there is that elite group of sluggers who have been ready when the pitch was fired. We painstakingly train our kids athletically to respond in a moment to any challenge before them, whether in basketball, baseball, football, or hockey.

But, when it comes to life's toughest decisions, often we don't prepare our kids for a proper response. Create several different hypothetical situations in which your children may find themselves with their peers or in the job market. Help them establish proper responses before they may need same.

Don't allow them to grope unprepared in a vulnerable moment. One good rule to teach them is: Do not act on impulse but take time to think the situation over. It is the same rule as in writing an important letter: Don't mail it the same day you wrote it. Wait until the next day. Read it. Rewrite it. Then mail it. Instantaneous acts cause us much difficulty. But teach your kids to apply all of the instructed principles of truth, honor, respect, and love in making those necessary quick decisions. In any kind of decision making, nothing will substitute for truth. The pitfall of being double-minded—which is vacillating about the truth—is one of man's greatest nemeses. It will destroy our kids.

If the parent is tuned in to the child's life and environment, creating these hypothetical situations will be easy. If not tuned in, the parent must begin at that point to learn of his or her kids' "everyday world." If the parents needs help, they should get books on the subject, talk to their teachers. consult their youth leaders, participate in their activities, attend school functions, read the newspaper, and so on. But, parents—get informed! Get involved! Get instruction! Get in tune with your kids if you want to inspire them to greatness.

13

Handling the Competition Within and Without

Each of our children is unique, with a unique capacity to conquer goals and even the world. We are indeed "more than conquerors through him Who loved us." When God created man he created him with the ability to dominate all the forces on earth. We must impart this information to our children and help them make their unique personal discoveries. Even a greater waste than the waste of the mind is the total waste of one's abilities, talents, and gifts.

While each child is unique in personal abilities, it is also true that each child will have his own unique deficiencies, so in this chapter let's first look at how to deal with our children's deficiencies. This is the first level of competition; it is the competition that goes on within ourselves as we seek to better ourselves and reduce our weaknesses and take ourselves up a notch. We must conquer our own deficiencies before we can conquer any outward competition. In the latter part of this chapter, we'll look at some specific considerations for helping our children to grow in their unique abilities to conquer their competition.

Overcoming your child's deficiencies— and your own!

The young man was excited beyond bounds after his Sunday school teacher led him to a saving knowledge of Jesus. It was only natural that he would want to join the church of the man who had led him to his new faith.

The Mount Vernon Church did not permit full membership without an oral examination by the pastor and deacons. When the young man stood in front of the committee, he was nervous and tongue-tied. Therefore, they rejected him from membership.

His deficiencies had reared their ugly heads! But before he was twenty-three, he had formed a Sunday school of 1,500 schoolchildren in the slums of Chicago. At twenty-eight, he became president of the YMCA and erected two buildings as well as two churches in Chicago.

In 1886 he founded what would later be named the Moody Bible Institute, the first Bible school of its kind in America. In the rustic 1800s he traveled over 1,000,000 miles spreading a message of hope and God's love for the century-old America and for Britain.

Who would question the spiritual validity of D. L. Moody? Moody was not deterred by his deficiencies. Instead, he overcame them and eventually spoke to more than 50,000,000 people about Christ; he led 1,000,000 to a saving faith. Moody was inspired to greatness in spite of his opposition—in spite of his deficiencies.

Everyone has them. Everyone has flaws. It's how we handle them that matters.

We've all seen and heard track athletes, mountain climbers, and other participants in individualistic sports. They give interviews on their recent efforts and are asked to comment about how they performed. Many

mes they will answer that they are pleased with their
erformance because they pushed themselves past their
nown limits. They bested their own personal records.
hey overcame their previously held deficiencies.

Indeed, there is a lesson here. Before we teach our
hildren to compete with others, we must teach them
ow to compete healthily with themselves. This, by and
arge, is a matter of teaching our children to conquer
heir own deficiencies and to turn their own weaknesses
nto strengths.

To do this, parents must help their children look
roperly at their own deficiencies. For that matter, can
ou as a parent accept the fact that your children have
weaknesses and deficiencies? It is essential that both
arents accept the premise that each child is not perfect.
How could they be, when each is the possible heir of
ach parent's imperfections and each grandparent's imperfections? Of the estimated 100,000 genes that a child
inherits, some are desirable. Some are undesirable. When
I consider the worst possible scenarios that each of my
children could inherit from me, my wife, my parents,
and my wife's parents, it frightens me to wonder what
each of my children could become. They could be
monsters!

Notwithstanding that Adamic syndrome they inherited from us, when you add it all up, the personality
possibilities are staggering and alarming. God probably
had mercy on all of us in regard to our children and their
heritage.

So just accept the fact that every kid has hang-ups and
problems that must be dealt with in order for him or her
to be competitive. The hardest thing for you may be
accepting that some of your children's hang-ups can be
directly traced to some of your own. We need to accept
that, too.

It is vital that we respond correctly to these special needs of our children. Therefore, when your children make mistakes or they have a problem, instead of shouting and degrading them, help them by:

1. *Recalling.* Recall a similar mistake in your own life when you were younger, and tell your child about it. (Watch him or her come alive by your identification and compassion.) To recall these experiences that we regret only proves to our children that we are sincere and humanly frail, the same as our kids. It shows that we are honest in our confession about our mistakes to our children. It proves that we are *real*, and not pretending, plastic phonies. Kids like honesty, sincerity, and realism in their parents. They respect it. And it helps them to accept their own shortcomings without taking on a load of guilt.

2. *Discussing.* Discuss the solution to the problem. Point out the consequences of the proble if it is not be properly dealt with. And note the blessing they will enjoy by overcoming their problem. Many parents concentrate on the problem by heaping guilt on the child. Many parents take the opportunity of their kids' mistakes to ridicule and degrade when the wise thing to do is simply to recount—not ridicule—the events, and then to rapidly proceed with a plan to discover the solution. It is imperative that the child accept the blame and responsibility for his or her errors and poor judgments. Do not enable them to pass the blame off on someone else. But get on with the solution to the problem.

3. *Laughing.* Laugh together about the situation. This may take some time. But remember that every problem is a disguised opportunity for solution. "A cheerful heart is good medicine, but a crushed spirit dries up the bones" (Prov. 17:22). If the child is remorseful and repentant, he

or she has likely already experienced much suffering over the incident. What the child needs now is support, understanding, and empathy. If it is appropriate for the occasion, the child needs laughter and joy and to know that every defeat in life can be turned into a victory if one is repentant and willing to surrender the situation to God.

4. *Befriending.* In the midst of a problem or difficulty, your kids and mine need a friend more than at any other time. They don't need a critic or a condemner. What they really need is someone who loves them despite the circumstances, someone who is "coming in the door of their lives" when everyone else is going out the door. Someone who says, "I'll be quiet, but I'll be right here to help you." It must be impressed on the child that during the rough times and all of the times in life, to get a friend our children must *become* friends! The reciprocity of friendship is beautiful. I want to be your friend. Will you be my friend? Nothing will stabilize a situation more than friendship.

5. *Sticking with them.* The test of friendship is time. It has no ending. It is forever if it is true friendship. It is a relationship to be cherished. It is a trustworthy companionship that has no limitations. It guarantees accessibility of one for the other. Sure, whenever we are faced with a problem we would like to snap our fingers and make everything okay immediately, but a majority of times it doesn't really happen that way. We generally don't get into our problems overnight, and often we don't get out of them overnight. Stick with your children until they succeed. Stick with them until they conquer their problems.

Conquering the outward competition

When our children have learned how to conquer their deficiencies, they can surely conquer the outward com-

petition. More than overcoming their inward competition—their own deficiencies—conquering the outward
competition begins with letting your children know that
they have the tools, support, and back-up system in their
parents and God to go all the way.

1. DISPEL FEAR—The greatest robber of one's ambition, goals, security, and happiness in life is fear. It is so
real that it can freeze a child in time and position and
keep him from pursuing life's challenges. Fear can cause
children (adults, too) to have nausea, delusions, or
imaginary enemies. It can destroy a person. A little over
a year ago a tragic incident happened near our residence.
Three twelve-year-old boys were having a camp-out in
their backyard one night. About 5:00 in the morning the
boys decided to walk to a convenience store because
they were hungry. Sad to say, one of the boys was
abducted and sexually abused. All the schools and
parents within several miles were contacted, and parents
were encouraged to explain to their kids what had taken
place and to share some safety tips to ensure that it
wouldn't happen to any other children.

We had no idea how this would affect our son, Jeremy,
who was ten at the time. He developed an overwhelming
fear of everybody he came in contact with. He didn't
want to ride the bus, didn't want to stay at school during
the day, and wouldn't stay overnight at friends' houses.
We got a call from his teacher at school that he was in
the bathroom sick and that maybe we should come to
the school and talk to him. So began a one-and-a-half
year journey with our son that Christie and I wouldn't
replace for anything in the world. Out of Jeremy's great
fear came a wonderful bonding with his parents that is
still going on today!

We cannot resolve our fears until we name and

acknowledge them and desire to solve them. The "solved" part of the problem situation implies breaking the fear up into parts, analyzing it, and reaching a decision—both at an individual and family level. We are always operating with a triangle:

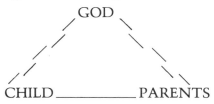

Coming to a solution means simply discovering the answer that would be compatible with and acceptable to God, the parents, and the child. It also means emphasizing that *no fear* is too large or too small that it can't be handled and solved in such a way that brings joy and peace to the entire family group represented in the triangle. The child must be convinced that there is no fear too significant or insignificant for the family team to consider together and arrive at a reasonable, practical, and satisfying solution.

When the parents ignore the child's little concerns, cares, or fears, the child becomes convinced in his or her mind that the parents would not be interested in his or her big fears in life. These days parents must be attentive to all areas of the child's life. A child can't go it alone. Life is too complex and critical. Our children need a support system standing by for dealing with everything that could present either good times or bad times.

We became Jeremy's support system throughout the next one-and-a-half years. We prayed with him several times during the day and night. We talked and talked and talked. We encouraged and praised him right through all his fears. We became Jeremy's full-time counselors, if you will.

My wife and her very good friend were conversing by phone the other day and this situation with Jeremy's fears came up at one point. She asked Christie why we didn't get professional counseling for Jeremy during this time in his life.

I must respond to her question by saying that no counselor could have done what we did for our son. We know him—and we know him even better now. This fear problem was a disguised blessing for our family.

Family life is not like it used to be! These days you can either give your children the attention, love, and consideration they deserve every day to overcome fears, or you can give it all after she is pregnant, he is on drugs, or they are in an auto accident or become members of a gang. Children will seek the attention, love, security, and consideration from some place to cope with their fears. It will be much better for all if they get these from their parents and family.

The difficulty is that children will *mask their fears* and not admit to a parent that they have any. Because of embarrassment and the feeling that their parents would not understand, they will conceal their fears. We were so grateful that Jeremy came to us.

Convince your children that you had fears when you were young and that you still have fears in adult life. It is normal to have fears, but *there is a solution to every fear.*

I repeat: Induce your children to *name* their fear and to *acknowledge* that they really have fears and want to find solutions. This is the beginning of dispelling fears.

In summary, first pray about the matter; then explore the realities of the fear; and then deduct the imagined, impossible, and unreal parts of the fear. Once this is done, the parents and children can design the instruction, training, and disciplines for overcoming it. *Involve God.*

2. INFUSE COURAGE—To flip the coin, the opposite of dismantling fear is creating courage. This is such a crucial area. Our kids cannot aspire to greatness without viewing *problems or deficiencies as opportunities* to be met with courage. This is what separates super-achiever children from those kids willing to settle with mediocrity.

We transmit courage to our children by *displaying* courage before them in the challenges we face as parents. Talk with your children about maintaining a *courage quotient*. Remind them that courage is not the absence of fear, rather it is the *will, determination*, and *commitment* to persevere. There will always be fear in a person's life. This fear can be channeled into preparation, prayer, and precepts, *if* the child is forewarned about fear being normal but solvable.

Courage is a preconceived attitude. The very best way to develop this attitude is to teach children to be proactive and not reactive. If only we can condition our children to believe that any task is accomplishable if approached creatively. Our efforts should be directed toward inducing our children to *approach* the issue from a positive view and not from a negative viewpoint; to be proactive and not reactive. In other words, we need to instill in our kids' minds that not only can they accomplish the goal but that they can do it *better* than anyone else.

Just remember that the basic rule for being courageous is to teach your child not to stand in awe of but to properly respect: (1) competition, (2) authority, (3) status quo, (4) politicians, (5) cultural elite, (6) media elite, (7) adversaries, (8) unknowns, or (9) problems.

To stand in awe of any of the those just mentioned or any other structure of power would *prevent* them from performing to their best potential. On the other hand, to stand in respect of any of the above will *prepare* them to perform at their best potential and to be creative in the approach to the issue.

Our contests in life are really not over after the fat lady has sung. If we keep trying and persevere, we will eventually succeed. To inspire your children to greatness and to tackle the outward competition is to equip them with emotions that stand in awe of no one or nothing except God.

3. TEACH CREATIVITY—Teach your children how to be creative. This is the forerunner to greatness. This is the edge our children will have on the competition. To be creative is to say that [I] will not work in the status quo, the mundane, the blasé, the ordinary, or the usual way that everyone does. Instead, [I] will develop a new and better way for my desired project. No one will convince me it can't be done until [I] have exhausted every moment and every method.

The basic rule of creativity is to take two or more known ideas, thoughts, plans, or programs, and combine them with that unique flavor that only your child can provide; then combine all of these parts into your newly created product or service to fill the niche or need that you had originally discovered in service or supply.

To inspire your kids to greatness, give your kids a chance to be creative. Begin early in their lives by exploring, venturing, and discovering a new, different and *better* way to do something—any task that interests them. Show them how to be creative about it. Parental involvement in all phases of your children's lives is essential if you want to inspire them to greatness. All phases would include education, arts, sports, church, studying, and so forth. You are always looking for a way to interest them in being creative. Anyone can be creative if inspired and motivated.

4. ENGENDER HOPE—The high suicidal ideation in our country is the result of an absence of hope among our kids. As parents we must breathe constant hope into our children, regardless if they fail a test, get cut from the team, or get rejected from the school play. Hope is what will keep them plodding along. Hope is desire with the expectation of fulfillment. Hope is what gets our kids started; courage is what helps them compete until they succeed.

5. CREATE CONFIDENCE—Confidence is our children saying in their minds, "I can do it"; "I know I can succeed"; "I have prepared and I am ready." Confidence is self-assurance and it does not come automatically. We instill it into our kids. They get it from us. As we recognize their accomplishments and continually praise them, they are accelerated with confidence to move to even higher levels of attainment and to defeat the competition.

Nothing grieves me more than having teenagers tell me that their parents always remind them that they will never amount to anything. Often, negative, disgruntled parents will repeatedly rehearse their children's past failures. What a supreme tragedy!

We have a silly custom in our home. Whenever one of our kids does something commendable, we clap for him or her. We don't politely clap; we roar our approval. Every single time it brings the biggest, broadest smile on our son or daughters' face. I know on the inside they are saying to themselves, "I did something right and everyone noticed. No challenge is too great for me!"

Many kids never succeed because they never try. So many of them have never been inspired to try. A large number of success stories are of people who tried and failed but never stopped trying. A part of winning is losing yet never being content with failure. By encouraging our kids we will enable them:

1. To venture out into any constructive, respectable pursuit in life.
2. To be brave in times of fear and danger.
3. To persevere in tasks that are difficult and painful.
4. To resist oppositions and confrontations in life while under total control of their faculties and emotions.
5. To hold their position when they believe they are right before the eyes of God.

We must ingrain in our kids the fact that there will always be competition. In athletics, academics, romance, and peer relationships let's help them to anticipate competition and to appreciate that it is healthy. Competition brings out the best in us. It helps us achieve greater levels of productivity.

6. ENCOURAGE REACHING FOR HIGH GOALS— Who should be better or more highly esteemed than people who have Jesus Christ living within? Through extended dialogue find out the interests of your son or daughter and help them from the beginning to reach for high goals of accomplishment. Inspire them to lead the class, to be the MVP on the team, to act as the problem-solver.

Magnify before them excellent role models in the fields of their interest. Because my son aspires to be a quarterback in the NFL, I continually point out to him the spiritual legends notable in the league. I watch the sports page for interviews with some of the very best who are Christians, and I read such excerpts of their reliance on Jesus Christ to Jeremy.

Help your children set the highest goals possible, realizing that they are only accomplishable through Christ. Jeremy and I recite together frequently Philippians 4:13, "I can do everything through him who gives me strength."

Quote it long enough and you will start to believe it.

Part of creating confidence in children is teaching them confidence that comes from understanding that they don't have to please everyone they meet. Helping them learn the proper approval priority will free our children to be confident in their performance and in their search for greatness. It will help them set the proper goals for seeking others' approval. Never forget the proper sequence: (1) God, (2) family, (3) self, and (4) others

The temptation is to seek approval of others first and selves second. This is a dangerous situation with our kids because it will warp their value system by substituting others' desires for their own.

Have you met these sad, insecure kids who constantly live for the approval of their friends? I have. They truly lack confidence. They are some of the emptiest young people I have ever been around. In the order of priority, we must instill in our kids' minds that the first one to consider for approval of our actions is God. Simply stated, will what I am considering doing please God? Is it in accordance with the Bible? Is it compatible with the teachings of my pastor or priest? If Christ were with me, would I perform that way? If the Holy Spirit is ever-present with me, can I perform this way?

After consideration is given to God's approval, I believe that each child should ask himself or herself: Would my parents approve of my conduct? Is my conduct compatible with the teachings of my parents? Would my parents vote yes or no about my action?

The last influence to consider for our actions is others' opinions. If we rely on others, we have become nothing but a puppet with our actions being determined by who pulls our strings and how our strings are pulled. Why does a child feel inclined to perform for the approval of others? Primarily because of the fear of: (1) rejection, (2) losing something, and (3) not fitting in.

This is exactly where Mom and Dad come in. We must build in our kids the fortitude—the confidence— to lead the pack, not follow it. The most effective way of doing this is helping them understand who they are in Jesus Christ. Every believer, young and old alike, has been given unique spiritual gifts at the moment of his or her new birth (Col. 3:77–12). When our kids understand that God has vested them with the talents to succeed, it doesn't really matter if they are "in vogue" with their friends. Help your son or daughter identify the spiritual gifts God has given to them.

Read 1 Corinthians 12 and Romans 12 and explain to your children the various gifts God has given to his people and why we are super-equipped when we discover them and use them to their fullest. Again, greatness is to be found in ordinary people who have discovered their extra-ordinary potential. Multibillionaire Sam Walton said, "There is absolutely no limit to what plain, ordinary people can accomplish . . . if they are given the opportunity and encouragement and incentive . . . [and] inspiration to do their best."

7. RUN THE RISK OF FAILING—It is imperative that we teach our kids that there will be failures in all areas of life, whether it is in our personal activities, our athletics world, our recreations. There will be failures! We will strike out a certain number of times. And we will hit singles, doubles, triples, and even some home runs in the pursuit of our goals in life.

Consider the man who hit 714 home runs. Did you also know that he struck out 1,330 times? But do we remember him for his successes or failures? The answer is obvious: his successes. For years Babe Ruth had been called the home-run king. But he was also a strike-out king. We remember him for his home runs. Most people don't even know about his poor strike-out performance. But he struck out almost twice as many times as he hit home runs.

So it is in life. Teach your kids that they will win some and lose some, but the game isn't over until the final at-bats in life. Every person who has experienced greatness in his or her life still must make that one final at-bat. We will all step into the batter's box with Jesus Christ as the umpire. I hope at that point that your kid will hit a home run when God throws the last pitch as he asks his Son, "Has this child made the most important decision of his life by trusting in you for his personal salvation?" I hope the answer is yes!

8. PROMOTE READING AND STUDY—Children need to read to be competitive. For some kids it is innate. Others need this habit taught to them. Help your child develop into a connoisseur of good books.

The greatest minister of England a century ago was Charles Haddon Spurgeon. His 15,000-member church was unheard of in London then and now! How interesting it is to view Spurgeon's library, which is now housed near my home at the William Jewel College in Liberty, Missouri. His 30,000 volumes point to the fact that Charles was an avid reader. What is so interesting is that he had books on a myriad of topics, not just theology.

9. PREPARE TO SERVE GOD—Since I became a Christian as a teen, I have always appreciated Ephesians 5:15, "Be very careful, then, how you live—not as unwise but as wise." As we said earlier, it bears

repeating that we must help our children prayerfully determine their future vocations as soon as possible and prepare for them. What an advantage on the competition to give our children early starts! In whatever area of life they are, teach them to serve God.

A few months after my conversion I knew I wanted to be an evangelist. My parents fostered the idea by encouraging me to speak at youth clubs in our metro area. Dad took me to Texas when I was fifteen to meet with a staff member of a well-known evangelist at the time. I started preparing evangelistic sermons to preach while I was still in high school. My parents were in total concert with what they felt was the longing of my heart.

Yes, some people don't discover their niches in life until later. Ray Kroc, the founder of McDonald's, was fifty-four years old when he opened his first fast-food hamburger store in Des Plaines, Illinois, but the sooner your child discovers his or her career choice, the better. Help your child by discussing many of the various vocations of life. Help your child to view many of the different career options available in our society.

Make the competitive commitment

You must teach your child that very little is accomplished in life without commitment. Commitment is not blind loyalty. It is not elitism. It is not authoritarian. It is not nonchalant or accidental. It is a result of beliefs, values, preparation, training, hard work, and creativity.

It is a determination to win without compromising integrity. It inspires both the child and others around the child. It is receptive to outside motivation. Its discipline is positive but never out of balance with a normal healthy life of emotions, spirit, mind, and body.

It is not totally isolated but does develop privacy to a

degree. Its fences are self-imposed, not mass controlled. It avoids going over the edge; it respects the dangers of the edge. It is balanced. It breeds satisfaction with the results and how the results were accomplished.

It is clinging to truth. It is always open communication. It is reverent to, and always inclusive of, God. It is determined to excel.

14

Loving and Forgiving Them

As we have seen throughout history, love is the most powerful motivator of humankind. We cannot lead our children to greatness without loving them. They must be overwhelmed with the surety of our love. We need to tell them *repeatedly* how much we love them. Love and forgiveness go hand in hand and are essential to our kids' success. A climate of love and forgiveness will be a magnet pulling them to us and away from destructive lifestyles.

Love talk

Let me recommend a language of love to which I know that your children will respond. Communicate these thoughts to them frequently:

1. I love you and accept you as you are.
2. I know you are valuable.
3. I desire what is best for you, not for me.
4. I hurt when you hurt.
5. I erase all offenses (from you to me).
6. I rejoice when I see you happy.
7. God's love for you exceeds mine.
8. I love you long term.
9. Time or difference will not stand between us.

Love is made up of muscle and guts, but it will never harm. Love is a device of advise and consent, never search and destroy. In the ever-changing cultural war into which we are thrust, love will never change or compromise. Love has two sides: the soft side (hugs) and the hard side (reproof/discipline). Developing both sides results in emotional balance. Love does not breed hostility; it instills hope.

By loving our kids we will stimulate them to reach for greatness. Our children need to know that no earthly love is greater than Dad and Mom's. With this foundation laid, we will be able to inspire our kids to greatness.

When kids do wrong in life, or make errors of judgments, and parents responds with "I forgive you and I love you," we warm their hearts. We bring a sparkle into their eyes and a breath of fresh air to their souls. We reverse a slow, painful death of their spirits. We inspire them to love themselves and forgive themselves instead of condemning themselves. There is no better medicine for a diseased psyche than to hear from your parent, "I love you and I forgive you."

The law and love

A young man was charged with embezzlement. His father was a respected Christian businessman well-known in the city and at his church. On the day of sentencing, the young man appeared before the judge, nonchalant and arrogant about his crime. He was hard and impenetrable. Father and son could not get along.

When the judge told the young man to stand up for the sentence to be read, a slight noise was heard on the other side of the courtroom. The young man turned toward the commotion and saw that his father was present and also arose to face the judge. His head and shoulders were bowed and stooped low in shame. He stood to be identified with his boy and to receive the verdict as if it were being pronounced on him.

Suddenly tears started to well in the son's eyes as he gazed at his dad with shame and contrition. Finally, he realized the grief he had inflicted on his father. It took the terrible courtroom experience to bring them together. This father loved and forgave his son.

And yet, who would ever believe that courts in America would ever consider, permit, or rule on a child suing his parents for divorce? Nothing could be so devilish and un-Christian. Our trends in America are dangerous. I hope all of Christendom is aware of the evil movement in America.

All the more reason to love our children even more deeply! Expressions of love are so reassuring to children. They convince them beyond a shadow of a doubt that you accept them even with weaknesses (sin). They are convinced that you, the parent, will not forsake, neglect, or divorce them, regardless of their actions.

Realistically, there will be times of discipline and failures. Essentially, we say by our many acts of love to our children: Remember, I want you to experience things in life that will bring to you joy, peace, and happiness. However, the disciplines are essential. I am commanded to discipline you as my child when you do wrong *because I love you and care for you.* I will do so without anger and in a spirit of love. And as your parent, I covet your counsel to me when you observe my doing wrong (sinning). I will stand corrected and submit to self-discipline. And certainly, society will discipline both of us (parent and child) for our respective violations in life. As long as the child realizes that the discipline is for correction and for proper punishment, he or she will be receptive of the discipline.

There are certain cruelties in life for children, certain issues that represent the height of lovelessness. The two worst are to not introduce your child to God and to not discipline your child. My dad always explained his disciplines to me and my four brothers in the most informative and intelligent way. And I knew he loved me all along. He said that if you have a problem in your life that needs discipline, there are four ways it can be accomplished:

1. I (Dad) can do it (the discipline).
2. The doctors (shrinks) can do it.
3. Law enforcement officers can do it.
4. You (the child) can do it.

Take your choice! Whom do you want to be your child's disciplinarian? Because if your child has a discipline problem, it will require *correction*. The easiest way will be for your children to correct themselves. The next best way is for the parent to take the helm and provide discipline. And from then on, take your choice: the shrink or the law. Every problem must be addressed by someone to prevent its becoming worse and destroying your life.

In my case, it was drugs and rebellion; and sure enough, as my dad said, "It almost destroyed my life."

No normal, sane, healthy parent wants to hurt or harm his child through discipline; but parents do want to correct problems. They want to because they love their children.

The endless, timeless rule of second chances

Yes, we discipline. And we always mix love with our discipline. One of the best ways to accomplish the healthy meshing of these two is by practicing the timeless rule of second chances. As parents we must impress on our children as early in life as possible that there are second chances, second opportunities, and second beginnings. If your child fails, makes a mistake, or has a problem, he or she can begin again, start over, and have another chance to succeed at whatever his or her endeavor is.

How many opportunities, chances, and beginnings do your children get? *As many as they need!* If your children get knocked down by life, they get a second chance if they get up. If they can't get up, the parent must make it absolutely known that he or she will always be present to reach down and help them get up. The opportunities and chances are endless as long as they have the resolve to keep on trying.

We must love our children as God loves us, with love that is always seeking to forgive and restore. Abraham was a liar—God gave him another chance. David was a murderer—God gave him another chance. Jonah was a runaway—God gave him another chance. Moses was a murderer—God gave him another chance. Paul was a persecutor—God gave him another chance. Matthew was a cheater and an extortioner—God gave him another chance. Mark was a failure—God gave him another chance. Peter was a liar—God gave him another chance.

The Bible is full of those average, normal, disobedient characters to whom God gave opportunity after opportunity to start over. The Bible is also full of so-called success stories of men and women who were prosperous on the outside but failed to accept their chance to start over; and their tragic endings are recorded.

Our kids need to be constantly affirmed in our love. I believe we must reiterate our love to them frequently.

Even Christian teens can develop massive problems if they doubt our deepest love for them.

Mandy's letter came to me recently. May her words never leave us as parents. "Dear Jerry," she wrote.

> *"I am seventeen years old and tried to commit suicide four times. The last time was the end of June, the night before my graduation ceremony. Most people wouldn't think that I'd be the one to commit suicide. I have been raised in a Christian family [and] have gone to church all my life. People see our family as a typical Christian family, one that is loving and kind with few difficulties. The truth is I've never heard my parents say they love me. I haven't heard those words for so long. I've almost forgotten what they sound like. I can't remember the last time someone gave me hug. I tried to kill myself by slitting my wrists. I so desperately need to know someone cares."*

Constantly affirm to your kids your undying love for them. Let them hear you say, "I love you," when they do good or bad, when their attitudes are great or pitiful. They must hear it from us before the brink of tragedy. Tell them today. Write it down and post it on their door; put it on their nightstand; slip it in their lunch. Tell them when they are alone, when they have failed, when they have won, and when they have lost. I wonder if Mandy would have ever raised a knife to her wrist if her parents had said, "We really love you." We must affirm our children with our love. We must give them second chances with our forgiveness.

15

Forging Family Covenants

In the beginning, God created his family team. Since that beginning there have been incidents and persons of failure, of success, and of greatness. But one fact remains: The family is still intact. Despite all of the obstacles, pitfalls, mistakes, errors in judgment, and sin, God's team will win.

What has kept God's family intact are the covenants or promises that God has made and kept throughout the ages. I believe in covenants and offer them for you to use in your family.

—VOLUNTARY FAMILY VALUE ETHICS CODE—

FAMILY NAME _____

DATE _____

Intent

The intent of this Family Value Ethics Code is to set forth an ethics code that identifies specifics that our family will strive to comply with, realizing that each of our family members leaves a "personal" and "family" fingerprint on each of their actions in life.

Family: Our family unit was created by God, and

therefore is very precious. It is to be appreciated, cherished, honored, and respected.

Values: Our value system is definite and specific, not abstract, fleeting, or subject to flippant or foolish pop cultural changes. Our values represent sensitivity to our God and our loved ones. Our values reflect our trust in our God and our families.

Our values are both our badge and our shield of life.

Ethics: We realize in these dangerous, perilous, and threatening times that our identification and definition of what is good and bad, right and wrong, moral and immoral, acceptable and unacceptable, is the foundation of our personal and family ethics.

To establish clearly our standard for ethics, our family has adopted God's Word as the basis of truth for our entire being.

Code: The word "code" is used instead of "rules" or "laws." This implies that the code is our goal, but unlike laws or rules, there are no penalties on the individual for violation of the code, other than self-imposed ones. A code by definition implies that it is entered into voluntarily, subscribed to voluntarily, with freedom for each individual member to withdraw anytime at his or her election without reprisal.

In Love: We covenant in this Family Value Ethics Code to convey to each other that we love each other and our Creator and that we are united as the only family in the world that bears our names, our relationships and our commitment to each other.

Signed _____ Date _____

Signed _____ Date _____

Signed _____ Date _____

Signed _____ Date _____

Signed _____ Date _____

Signed _____ Date _____

—THE FAMILY TEAM COVENANT—

FAMILY NAME _____

DATE _____

We, the undersigned members of the Family Team Covenant, do on this date, make perpetually effective for the remainder of our lives the following:

I. We are united as a family team by birth or adoption and by the will of God.

II. We will exhibit toward each other, separately and collectively, *agape*, love that is unconditional.

III. We will exercise forgiveness and trust toward each other.

IV. We will agree that all members must be mindfully and respectfully obedient to God's laws.

V. We will agree to submit to the authority of man's laws so long as they do not contradict God's laws.

VI. We will try to be good citizens in respect to our governments and to serving our fellow man in need.

VII. We will apply our gifts, talents, and abilities to the best of our ability, always reaching to greatness.

VIII. We will, as a team, inspire each other, help each other, and make ourselves available in all areas of life. To do so, we will always maintain our principles and God's truths, and we will not compromise either.

IX. We make this covenant voluntarily and allow anyone to withdraw at any time without reprisal.

Signed _____ Date _____

Signed _____ Date _____

Signed _____ Date _____

Signed _____ Date _____

Signed _____ Date _____

Signed _____ Date _____

—FAMILY BILL OF RIGHTS—

FAMILY NAME _____

DATE _____

Our Family Bill of Rights is very brief and simple. Each family member, regardless of age, is important and has the right to be seen, to be heard, to be considered in family decisions, to be protected from inside and outside abuse or harm, and to be trained, informed, and inspired to greatness.

Our family will have rules that are fair and equitable and that provide forgiving relief for any violation thereof. Our family is glued together with love and respect and not hard rules that are difficult or severe. Our rules are designed to instruct and protect, not to punish. It is imperative that our Family Bill of Rights be properly told, explained, and demonstrated to each family member, establishing the boundaries, rewards, and disciplines for all.

Although our individual rights are of immense importance, the rights of our family and God must also be considered. In many cases we will each consider voluntarily surrendering our individual rights to our God, who has established only those rights for us that are fair and impartial.

Signed _____ Date _____

Signed _____ Date _____

Signed _____ Date _____

Signed _____ Date _____

Signed _____ Date _____

Signed _____ Date _____

These documents state simply our position as a family. They are voluntary. They can be withdrawn at any time, by any member. In the legalistic times that we live in, our covenants will portray to ourselves and the world that, as families, we are steadfast.

I recommend that each family read and study the covenants. Only after discussion should a family agree and subscribe to them. Why do I recommend covenants? Because God has covenants throughout the Bible. Covenants take out the indefinites and supply the definites. In our lifetime and the lifetime of our kids, we all want to aspire for greatness, because the opposite is failure.

And failure can make a person feel as if he or she is in a pit, never to be gotten out of.

In every area of life, *teams win; individuals lose.* We see it every day on television in the sports world. Stars and superstars don't win as teams. But teams, including the bench and substitutes, win. For the coach it is a matter of blending the abilities, talents, gifts, egos, personalities, and chemistries of all of the individuals into a team.

This is the same job for the parents of any family. Because in a family, individual members don't singularly fail or succeed. They do either as a team.

16

Storing Up Prayer for Them

Hannah was provoked by her adversary continually because she did not have a child. She wept, fasted, and prayed year after year without answer. Her husband tried to comfort her with his profound love for her. She continued to pray so long that she was in bitterness of soul. Still no answer came to her agonizing prayers. She continued to weep and did not eat. She continued to pray for a child to be born to her because she was barren of child. So she vowed to the Lord, "Lord Almighty, if you will . . . give [me] a son, then I will give him to the Lord for all the days of his life" (1 Sam. 1:11).

God then answered her prayer. She gave birth to a child and called his name Samuel, because she had asked him of the Lord. After the child was weaned, she took him to the house of the Lord, where he would live the rest of his life. She kept her vow to God. Hannah then prayed her prophetic prayer to the Lord, emphasizing the holiness of God. Her greatly inspired prayer is recorded in 1 Samuel 2 to memorialize Hannah and her prayer forever. For a child to be inspired to greatness, as Samuel was, he or she must have parents who pray as Hannah did. Furthermore, I am sure that as Samuel grew up, he was inspired himself to pray by the example of his mother.

To attain to greatness for your children, adopt the Hannah method of praying!

There is no force greater in life than prayer. A person could read this entire book and agree with its principles, but if that parent doesn't pray, then there will be little greatness. There will be no power behind the principles.

On the other hand, one of the reasons we are ending with this chapter is because of the hope it offers. Is there any reader who is overwhelmed by the challenge and information I've offered in this book? That's understandable. But the good news is that with prayer, there is no need to be overwhelmed. With prayer, we can tap into the divine power of God that will enable us to achieve the challenge of inspiring our kids to greatness.

Prayer is unleashing a power that will provide forces to overcome evil, surpass ordinary expectations, and supersede the natural into realms of supernatural activity. Prayer is the vehicle that mobilizes God and all of his angels to serve the believer.

Prayer petitions are heard by God and make him want to act on behalf of the faithful. And devoted prayer will make your child great.

One of the greatest basic proofs of the omniscience of God is his ability to hear every single prayer in the universe. How could hundreds of millions of prayers per twenty-four-hour period be heard and acted upon by someone who is not omniscient? The logistics are staggering, even beyond comprehension by mere natural man.

Now, to inspire our kids to greatness and to prepare them and equip them to handle traumatic, unexpected events in their lives as if nothing has happened, it is compulsory that we store up prayer for them. A wise parent will not only have daily A.M. and P.M. prayers for his or her kids but will take every additional opportunity to store up prayer.

The fruits of prayer

The last encounter Andy Lauer had with his fifty-eight-year-old dad, Lester, before Lester died was when Father led his family gathering during a send-off time of Bible reading and prayer for sister Becky and Andy, who were about to go on a mission trip. Becky, Mom Dixie, Andy, and his dad hugged and told each other they loved one another. The Lauer family had performed this ritual many times.

Every kid in America would want a father like Lester.

Lester believed in "stored-up prayer." Because he had been a fire fighter for twenty-five years, he was a light sleeper. The slightest noise, it seemed, could awaken him. Insomnia was a common problem. What did he do on those nights when he could not rest?

"My dad would read his Bible and intercede for my future and for Becky's. He would store up prayer," says Andy.

People could always count on Lester to pray; when they had a need, it seems many people went to him.

On that final day during the send-off time of Bible study, Lester read out of his *One Year Bible*. For some reason, Lester actually read about a week ahead in the chronology he was following. The day's reading he chose was June 23. Andy would not learn the significance of that date until later.

The family had sacrificed for Andy and Becky to join the church's mission trip to Mexico. It was something Andy was raring to do. Earlier at the Nazarene National Youth Congress, Andy explained that he had been fighting with God about his future. "I wanted a vocation that would make more money than the ministry. I wanted to be well-off and enjoy nice things. I have always liked nice things."

But God won the battle. Before he left for the mission trip, Andy surrendered to the Lord and sensed a particular call to evangelism. No wonder he was flying high on the trip. It was similar to an inspiring movie, *The Mission*, which he had seen.

He had even shared with the other kids on the trip his faith in Christ during camp devotions. Andy spoke in a way that moved and captivated his young audience. One day he had been working in the hot Mexican sun and upon returning to the hotel, he showered and was hungry for dinner. The date: June 23.

Youth leader Dave Sharpe seemed nervous in the lobby as he chewed on the interior of his lip.

"Andy, your parents have been in a wreck. Your dad is dead," Dave told him.

Apparently Andy did not hear the last part—"Your dad is dead."

Amidst tears Andy asked Dave, "What did you say about my dad?"

"He's dead," Dave replied. Andy had been slated to say a few words at devotions that night. Dave knew that was out of the question now. Plans were underway to get Andy and Becky back home for the funeral. Yet it was Andy who insisted on speaking to the youth group that evening.

Earlier in the day he had read, "because you know that the testing of your faith develops perseverance. Perseverance must finish its work so that you may be mature and complete, not lacking in anything" (James 1:3–4). James was his favorite book.

During the devotion, Andy told the kids, "Even though my dad is gone, I still love God with all of my heart. Nothing has changed!"

The impact of his talk was immeasurable!

Why did Lester read from the June 23 entry, which

turned out to be the day he died? Why that day in Iowa did he miss the turn to the motel? Why did the other driver reach down for something and swerve the wheel causing both cars to hit, head-on at fifty-five miles per hour? Those answers only God really knows. But I know this: God answered Lester's persistent prayers for the spiritual growth of his son.

Two weeks after the incident, on the local Christian TV show, "Straight Talk," Andy shared his testimony and ended the show by staring into the camera and explaining the Good News of Jesus Christ to the audience. One thing is certain: Andy Lauer is going on for God, a radiant Christian. His light shines brightly. He is now in a Christian college preparing for the ministry.

Lester and Dixie did many things right as parents. Things that we'd all do well to note. Andy has been inspired to greatness. Lester's prayers were at the bottom of it all.

What to pray for

You can inspire your kids to greatness also. As parents the greatest thing we can do for our kids is pray for them as Lester did. Because I am away from home so often, I find it comforting to pray for my kids throughout the day. Even mounted on a high-school platform before a couple thousand kids, I pray for Danielle, Jeremy, and Jenilee. In bed at night, in a loud hotel, I lift them to the Lord.

What should we pray for regarding our children? In my estimation, these are the urgent areas:

1. Personal salvation experience (2 Tim. 3:15).
2. Active continual spiritual growth (2 Peter 3:18).
3. Healthy physical development (Luke 2:52).
4. Future mate (Prov.18:22).

5. Discovery of personal gifts and talents (Eph. 3:7–8).
6. Moral and spiritual purity (Eph. 5:3).
7. Vibrant relationship with parents (Deut. 5:16).
8. Achievement of greatest dreams/goals (Ps. 37:4).
9. Love for God (Deut. 6:5–6).
10. Long life (Eph. 6:2–3).
11. Humility (Prov. 22:4).
12. Success (Josh.1:8).
13. Strength during temptation (1 Cor. 10:13).
14. Good study habits (2 Tim. 2:15).

No parent fully comprehends the impact he or she is making every day when praying. Let me make a suggestion. After reading this book, get down on your knees. Acknowledge your need for God's help to inspire your children to greatness. If you like, you can pray this prayer as a starter:

Lord, you are great and you have called your children to follow you into greatness. But the task is too big for me alone. Father, please guide me and strengthen me as I try to parent my children to greatness. Let me love them, discipline them, and teach them. And when it is all said and done, let me release them into your hands as ready and usable servants, trusting you to fashion greatness out of them for your kingdom. In Jesus' name, amen.

We can pave the way for our kids' greatness by our prayers!

17

Afterword

I want to address two concerns in closing.

Never, never, never give up!

First, I want to leave you with a word of hope. Are you worried about the past? Do you feel you've "botched" your children up to this point? Don't succumb to this kind of thinking. Today you can start inspiring your children to greatness. This is one of the greatest facts of the Christian life. We can change, and with God's help, we can begin again. There is always hope!

Don't stop hoping in your children. You may, in fact, be committed to inspiring your children to greatness, but everyone around you sees nothing great in your child. Don't let the opinions of others discourage you. Consider the following story:

William loved Emily Regina Cavanaugh, who was one grade ahead of him in school. They were engaged to be married and William was overwhelmed with his love. But one spring, she broke the engagement. A friend speculated later on the reason: "She wanted to marry a man that was going to amount to something and didn't think he was going to make it. I will never forget that. We figured that she was right. It so broke him up. I think that was a big turning point. He just got down and asked the Lord to really give him something he could hold on to."

Two years earlier, William had been feeling sick and

out of place at the Christian college he was attending. The well-known founder of the college personally told him, "If you leave and throw your life away at a little country Bible school, the chances are you'll never be heard of. At best, all you could amount to would be a poor country Baptist preacher somewhere out in the sticks."

Such were the feelings of two important people in William's life. People wrote William off. They thought he would not attain greatness.

But Billy Graham has become the yardstick for godly greatness.

Don't ever write your children off. And don't listen to anyone who does! Greatness is defined at the end of the race, not the beginning.

What about your personal greatness?

Finally, the one who has been given the greatest things in life but who fails can be considered the greatest failure in life. Many great ones fail every day. Wealthy people fail. Famous people fail. Powerful people fail. Successful people fail. Great achievers fail.

As I made clear in chapter 1, you cannot attain true greatness if you have not answered the most basic question, "Where will I spend eternity?" Biblical greatness ultimately means kingdom greatness. So if you are not a follower of the King, in the end you cannot be great.

Preparing for eternity prepares us for the challenges of everyday life. What good are life and any material possessions if you die unprepared to meet God?

I know a way that you can be ready. A young man named Adoniram Judson found that way, and the way he found it is one of the most curious stories I have ever heard.

Adoniram Judson was the first American to become a foreign missionary in the late 1800s. Missiologists regard him as the one who pioneered the concept of an American's leaving U.S. soil and going to the foreign field with the message of redemption.

Adoniram was born in a Congregational minister's home. At age five, his father was already teaching him to read the Greek New Testament. Later he left home and went to Brown University, now one of America's most prestigious universities. Judson attended Brown during the French Revolution when the air was filled with agnosticism and skepticism. His roommate was named Ernest. Despite his father's early teaching, Adoniram and his friend Ernest went through college as unbelievers and when they graduated neither were interested in Christian things. Eventually they parted company.

Later in life, Judson was riding on horseback when night came. He pulled into a village that had only one inn in the town, but it was full. The innkeeper said, "We have no room except one little room. Next door there is a man dying, and he is yelling and screaming all the time." Said Judson, "I am so tired and sleepy it makes no difference to me. Go ahead and give me that room."

He tied his horse up and entered his room. Judson heard the voice in the next room. Sometimes the person would plead with God for mercy—other times he would curse God in rage. Finally, during the night, the voice stopped and Judson fell asleep.

The next morning as he was paying his bill, Judson asked the innkeeper, "Whatever happened to the man next door?"

"Well," the innkeeper responded, "Last night he died."

"What was his name?" Judson asked casually.

"His name was Ernest." It had been his old roommate—Ernest—with whom he had gone to Brown University.

Judson staggered to his horse dazed. Every time the horse's hooves hit the hard ground, two words kept running through his mind:

—DEAD, LOST. DEAD, LOST—

He turned around and went home. Judson invited Jesus Christ in his life and went to Andover Seminary and ultimately to the country of Burma. God gave him a mission. He knew that Christ was in his heart and he had a message to tell.

Adoniram escaped the fate of his friend. His friend ultimately failed. But Adoniram went on to godly greatness.

Ultimate failure and success

The greatest failure in life is you, if you are not a believer. All else will seem so minor compared to this failure in life—to be lost forever, separated from the God of the universe.

All other accomplishments will be of little importance to your life if you fail in this decision. This decision, the greatest of all, must be singular and personal. No one can make it for you. Only you will determine and decide your standard and standard bearer.

As parents, and as kids, we are each called by God for greatness. I know that we and our kids will each aspire to greatness. But don't fail in the chief criteria of achieving greatness.

From this reading, as parents you have been given much of the information for inspiring your kids to greatness. It is my hope and prayer that all of you succeed. Of necessity, it begins and ends with your knowing Christ and confessing him as your Lord, Savior, and Master. Remember what George Whitefield said: "You can only lead someone [your child] as far as you yourself have gone." If you haven't begun your travels down the path of life with Christ, do it now.

If you make your decision for Christ, write to me for the same helpful literature that we give to the people in our crusades. Also, I desire any information that you are willing to provide about how you have inspired your kids to greatness. Write me a letter and tell me your personal accomplishments. Advise me if you want me to treat your stories confidentially or to publish them to help others. Together we can inspire our kids to greatness! Simply write to:

Jerry Johnston

Personal Time Cycle Chart

TIME SPENT:							
DATE:	**Mon.**	**Tue.**	**Wed.**	**Thu.**	**Fri.**	**Sat.**	**Sun.**
Sleeping							
Eating							
Working							
Traveling							
With Family							
With Wife							
Privately . . . 　—With #1 Child							
—With #2 Child							
—With #3 Child							
Watching TV							
Personal Recreation							
Family Recreation							
Exercise							
Reading Bible							
Praying							
Worshiping							
At Church							
With Pets							
With Friends							
On the Phone							
Reading Papers							
Magazines, Books							
Other							
TOTAL							

Parent Sweetness Test

Develop a "sweet" relationship toward the child
Circle 1 (least) through 5 (most).

a.	Loving	1	2	3	4	5	n.	Amiable	1	2	3	4	5
b.	Pleasant	1	2	3	4	5	o.	Sensitive	1	2	3	4	5
c.	Pure	1	2	3	4	5	p.	Helpful	1	2	3	4	5
d.	Gentle	1	2	3	4	5	q.	Shares time	1	2	3	4	5
e.	Tender	1	2	3	4	5	r.	Forgiving	1	2	3	4	5
f.	Empathetic	1	2	3	4	5	s.	Smiling	1	2	3	4	5
g.	Charming	1	2	3	4	5	t.	Humorous	1	2	3	4	5
h.	Fun	1	2	3	4	5	u.	Shares info.	1	2	3	4	5
i.	Wholesome	1	2	3	4	5	v.	Joyful	1	2	3	4	5
j.	Sympathetic	1	2	3	4	5	w.	Sincere	1	2	3	4	5
k.	Kind	1	2	3	4	5	x.	Shares poss.	1	2	3	4	5
l.	Considerate	1	2	3	4	5	y.	Friendly	1	2	3	4	5
m.	Pleasing	1	2	3	4	5	z.	Attentive	1	2	3	4	5

If your total score is 130–100, you are super sweet
If your total score is 99–70, you are really sweet
If your total score is 69–40, you are sort of sweet
If you total score is 39–1, you are a little sweet